Traveling High
and
Tripping Hard

By Joseph Davida

DARK PLANET PRESS

Front cover design and illustrations by Travis Gillan
Back cover design by Samantha Starr

This is a memoir and contains some autobiographical
elements about the author. The author has made every
attempt to recreate events, locales, and conversations
from his memories of them. In order to maintain their
anonymity, the author may have changed or may have
left out the names of individuals, places, and
identifying characteristics and details such as physical
properties, occupations, and places of residence.

PUBLISHED BY DARK PLANET PRESS

ISBN- 0-9993975-0-8
ISBN-13: 978-0-9993975-0-3
First Edition

for my father

LONG ISLAND

I grew up in a small working-class town near the Queens-Nassau county border. Technically, it was an incorporated village. Even though it was less than twenty miles from Manhattan, the town maintained strict zoning laws that were designed to keep the modern world at bay. There were no fast-food chains, franchises, or department stores. The main road had a strip of mom-and-pop-owned businesses that provided all of the essentials. In theory, you could live out your entire life without ever having to leave. There were a few small restaurants and bars…a butcher, a baker, and a grocery store. There was a post office, a pharmacy, and a bank. An old two-screen movie theater and a bowling alley. The town had its own police department, and even the last operational farm in Nassau County. Everyone knew everyone else. All the kids referred to the town as Mayberry.

I lived on a street called Wright Avenue. Every day, I walked to and from school with a kid named Jay who lived a few doors down from me. He was my best-friend-slash-arch-enemy. After school, we usually stopped at one of the candy stores that we passed on our walk back home. Either Lenny's or Mike's Lotto. Both places were pretty much unchanged since the 1940s. They each had racks of newspapers and magazines up against the walls, candy displays, and cartons of cigarettes on the shelves behind the register. They also both had long wooden counters equipped with old-fashioned soda fountains and round spinning seats bolted to the floor.

One afternoon in 1984, Jay and I decided to stop at Mike's. The store had recently acquired the new Elevator Action arcade game, and we were anxious to play it. After putting a quarter in the machine, we took turns sharing lives, then walked over to the counter to buy candy with whatever coins we had left. Since you could get more candy by buying the pieces individually, I usually bought some Dubble Bubble bubblegum and probably a few loose Peanut Chews or Mary Janes. The bubblegum came wrapped in waxy pieces of paper, the ends twisted like a Tootsie Roll. I vaguely remember that one of the pieces had an abnormal amount of bitter-tasting powdered sugar (that's supposed to keep the gum from sticking to the paper), but after over thirty years it's hard to say for sure.

After inhaling our candy, we rushed home to pick up our cleats and gloves for Little League practice. As we walked over to the field behind the junior high school, I began to notice that things were starting to look a little strange. Everything seemed to be taking on unusually vivid colors, and normally inanimate objects seemed to be pulsating with energy. By the time I made it to the baseball diamond, practice was already underway and I was rushed onto the outfield with my mitt. I don't know how long I was out there, but I remember staring at the trees in the distance...and for some reason, the leaves appeared to be spinning.

The next thing I knew, I was up at bat. Justin Calabria, who I didn't like at all, was winding up to throw out a pitch. As I watched the ball come flying in my direction, I thought I detected something sinister...something about the way it whizzed past me over the plate. But it wasn't until I saw the next pitch coming that I knew for sure. Somehow, in midair, that ball transformed into a missile...kind of like the ones Wile E. Coyote buys from the Acme Corporation. And then my suspicions were confirmed: Justin Calabria was trying to kill me. Then, as if a switch went off, something in me snapped, and I realized that I had to destroy him—before he could destroy me.

I started running toward the mound with the bat clenched tightly in my hands, and chased him into the outfield with the sole intent of smashing in his face! When the coaches realized what I was trying to do, they chased after me and eventually began to close in from all sides. Every time they tried to get close, I swung my bat at them with all the force I could possibly exert.

My father was an assistant coach for the team and he would sometimes show up a little late for weekday practices. Out of the corner of my eye, I saw that his car had just pulled into the parking lot, and I heard Coach Evans yell out to him, "Hey Al, your son has gone fuckin' crazy!" I froze as I saw my dad running toward me. He slowed down as he got close, and the other coaches stepped back. As he approached, my fear started to melt away. He pulled the aluminum bat out of my hands, and kneeled down and grabbed me by the shoulders. He looked directly into my eyes and could apparently see that my pupils were completely dilated.

He said, "He hasn't gone crazy…he's tripping his fucking brains out."

At the time, I didn't know what that meant. I was only eight years old.

***

I don't remember everything that happened after leaving the baseball field, but I know at some point after getting home my father had me piss into a cup. He sent my urine out with one of our neighbors, who worked as a lab technician at the local hospital. Fortunately, after having his own experiences with psychedelics in the 1960s, my dad was smart enough to realize that taking me to the hospital might not be the best idea.

After the lab analysis was completed, a doctor called the house and told my parents that I had tested positive for PCP. While no one had any idea where it had come from, the doctor said that I'd somehow ingested a very large dose…enough to potentially cause a psychotic breakdown in a full-grown adult. The only thing they could possibly do was give me a large shot of Thorazine, but apparently the amount needed to counter my hallucinations came with its own set of risks. In some kind of bizarre experiment, my dad decided the best thing he could do was let me ride it out.

***

When night fell, my father took me up to my room and put me to bed. After tucking me in, he turned off the light and told me to try to sleep. It wasn't long after he left the room that things began to get *really* weird. First, the walls burst into flames, and then the floor started oozing blood and lava. I looked up and noticed demonic bat-like creatures flying around the ceiling. I knew where I was…and it was hell. Suddenly, a shadowy figure started rising out of the molten ground, and began to materialize right in front of me. He looked straight at me and I asked him who he was.

"Who are you?" I said.

Without making a sound, the creature spoke directly into my brain, answering in German—which, to my surprise, I could understand perfectly: "You *know* who I am."

He was right. I did know who he was.

Then I asked him why I was there and again he answered me telepathically: "You know why you are here…"

"No," I replied. "I don't!"

But I did know, I thought. It was because I was evil.

The figure started laughing. "Yes, that is right! You *are* evil!"

I asked what he wanted from me, and the fiend quickly morphed into a form that looked familiar. It was Hitler. I knew it was him because both of my grandfathers had been in the war.

He was smiling, and then he answered me: "You know what we want you for. You were chosen! You are going to finish my work for me and take over the world!"

"But I'm only eight years old," I said. "How am I supposed to take over the world?"

Yet even before he could reply, I knew the answer: I had to kill my parents.

***

By the time my father came back into my room to check on me, I had already resigned myself to my terrible fate. I was sitting on my bed in the dark, staring into the infernal abyss, with an open Cub Scout pocketknife in hand. When my dad turned on the light, he could see that some really bad shit was happening.

"Umm... What's going on, man?"

"Dad. I'm evil. I just spoke with the devil and he told me that I have to kill you and Mom to take over the world."

Now that I am a parent myself, I can't even imagine how I would have dealt with a situation like that. But this is why my father was the man. It is almost impossible to fully comprehend how delicate my psyche was at that point, but what my father said was perfect. He told me that not only was I not evil, I was in fact a pretty good kid. He said I was being tested, and only if I gave in and actually killed my mother and him would I become evil. Even in my semi-deranged state of mind, this seemed to make sense.

After seeing how quickly things went south when I'd been left alone, my dad decided not to take any more chances. He asked me to hand him the knife, and then took me downstairs to lie down in his bedroom. For the next few hours, I saw the history of the universe play out before my eyes— from the Big Bang up to the rise of modern civilization. And then, I witnessed what I could only perceive as the future...and it looked grim. The world was at war: cities were burning, children were starving, and entire populations were killing one another. It seemed like the entire planet was possessed by madness. The entire surface of the Earth was either devastated by drought or flooded with water. It was the apocalypse, the end of the world, and I could see that it would happen in my lifetime.

Then there was only death—and everything went dark.

Just when I thought it was finally all over, the

room became engulfed in an almost blinding white light. I could hear a sound—a constant layering of notes played by an orchestra of unknown celestial instruments—that climaxed when it reached a perfect chord. And then…I heard a voice. It was the sweetest voice I had ever heard, and it told me that I'd passed my test…that my heart was pure. And then it explained that while everything I'd seen was real, it was not too late. There was still time for things to turn out okay, but there was just one catch…

I had to save the world.

I called out to my father, who was sitting outside the door: "Dad, you were right! An angel came and told me it's going to be okay!"

I was crying hysterically, but these were tears of joy. The gravity, the weight of my mission was not yet apparent, but at that point it didn't matter…the nightmare I had been experiencing for fourteen hours was coming to an end. All I felt was an overwhelming sense of relief, and for the moment at least, I knew it was all over. Then, finally, I fell asleep.

HOLLAND

In the summer of 1994, I was living in a dilapidated piece-of-shit apartment on the Lower East Side of New York City. I had moved in a year earlier, after the lease on my previous apartment in the West Village expired. Technically I was subletting it from a guy named O'Brien, but in actuality he had just pocketed my rent and security deposit. I found out only a few weeks after moving in, when a Hasid, who was acting as the building manager, told me that O'Brien was in the process of getting evicted.

He wanted me to pay him the rent directly, but the other tenants told me that he would just wind up pocketing my money too. The whole place was filled with junkies who weren't paying rent, and the ownership was changing hands so often that no legal procedures were actually ever getting done...instead, the building just wound up being juggled by a bunch of different banks that wanted nothing to do with it.

Clinton Street, between Stanton and Rivington, was right in the heart of the heroin district. It was once part of the Jewish ghetto, back when Meyer Lansky was still running numbers—but at the time it was primarily a Hispanic neighborhood, with only a handful of white degenerates, musicians, and thieves who couldn't afford to live anywhere else. Salsa music was blasted constantly—through car stereos, boom boxes, and transistor radios—the steady rhythms only disrupted by the occasional gunshot.

Apart from a couple of bodegas and a botánica where they sold candles and Santeria spells, the block was mainly residential. The corner by my apartment had an empty lot that had been transformed into a "garden" that mainly consisted of overgrown weeds and, of all things, chickens. The first night I slept in the apartment, I woke up to a rooster crowing. A fucking rooster...in Manhattan. This was before Giuliani had the nerve to start enforcing a no-domestic-farm-animal policy in his attempt to clean up the city.

Eventually, NYU bought up most of Clinton Street and turned it into a nice little gentrified neighborhood filled with dormitories, boutiques, and coffee shops, but back then the only real commerce being conducted was by the heroin dealers. They were stationed every twenty to thirty feet, standing on every available corner, in every doorway, and at every payphone, each pushing their own brand of dope. "Poison, Poison," "Body Bag, Body Bag!" or shouting out, "I got works!"

After a year of essentially squatting in

apartment 2B rent-free, I found out that a new bank had taken over the building and hired a management company that actually seemed serious about cleaning up the place. One day, a nervous-looking man in a suit and tie came banging on my door and offered me the chance to sign a new lease. With the city marshal standing behind him, he told me that if I didn't sign and start paying rent, the new owners would begin the eviction process. I guessed that meant he liked me because most of the other tenants just woke up to find "vacate immediately" notices on their doors. Either way, I knew time was running out.

I had the money to pay the rent, but just wasn't sure I could stick it out for another year. The whole neighborhood was taking its toll, and I figured my best bet was to try and get out of there while I still could. While the rational side of me knew that I should probably start looking for a new apartment, I decided to use what little money I had to buy a plane ticket to Amsterdam instead.

***

The reason I chose to go to Holland, of course, was for the weed. I had read all about the high-grade strains of herb that were sold in their coffee shops, and after a few years of selling weed in New York, decided it would be a nice change of pace to be the customer for once. In the States, I wasn't even technically old enough to buy a beer, so the thought of being able to smoke a joint in public

11

without having to look over my shoulder seemed like the greatest thing in the world.

I found a cheap flight in the back of the *Village Voice* that was set to leave in a week. Right after I bought the ticket, I realized that I was also going to need a new passport. The one I had was from a trip to Italy I had taken with my family as a kid, and it had just expired. In the mid-1990s, if you had an existing ticket, the passport agency at Rockefeller Center could issue you a new one quickly. I moved my girlfriend, my dog, some records, and my musical equipment into one of our friend's apartments on First Avenue and packed up my shit. I was eighteen years old and pretty excited about traveling out of the country on my own for the first time. A few days later, I took a cab to JFK and boarded a plane.

On the flight over, I studied a travel guide for Western Europe that I'd picked up in the airport. I looked over the list of hostels in Amsterdam, and found one that was attached to a club called the Melkweg. The fact that it was cheap and also had a coffee shop probably sealed the deal. After landing in Schiphol, I exchanged some dollars for guilders and bought a train ticket to Centraal Station. On the ride over, I noticed that the landscape looked a whole lot bleaker than any Van Gogh painting, and immediately understood why they'd legalized the weed. If it hadn't been, I could see how people might get tempted to start cutting off their own body parts. It wasn't until the train passed a few windmills that I began to have any sense of

Holland's unique charm.

By the time I got into town, it was early morning and I was pretty shot from not sleeping on the flight. I asked someone the best way to get to the Melkweg and was directed in perfect English—better English than I spoke myself—to the subway station. I remember being impressed with the electronic ticketing system, since New York was still using tokens at that point. Just a few minutes later, I reached my stop, and quickly realized that Amsterdam was a lot smaller than I had imagined.

***

The hostel looked like a mutiny had taken place inside a coed army barracks. There were bunk beds everywhere, and backpacks full of shit were strewn all over the place. Most of the people were European, and they had sectioned off areas based on their country of origin. I assumed that the war was still fresh in the European psyche because even after fifty years, the Germans still seemed to be shunned by everyone.

After finding a bed, I threw my bag in a locker and went down to the café. I was exhausted, but knew there was no way I could fall asleep before buying some weed. I went up to the counter and grabbed a menu of various Indicas and Sativas, imported hashes, and baked goods of every variety. It was a teenage pothead's dream. With wonder, I looked everything over, and decided on a few grams of their best weed, along with two different types of hashish. Good hash was hard to come by in New York, so I bought a dark and chocolatey Indian Manali and some blonde Charas. The Dutch usually smoke their weed with tobacco, so, as I was rolling up a huge joint filled with straight weed and hash, someone gave me a look like I was the guy who orders a pint of tequila his first time at a bar. But I didn't give a shit; I wanted to get stupid.

The hostel had a little yard in the back, and after messing around with my guitar for a bit, I laid down on the grass and took a nap. A few hours later, I was woken up by a kid with green and purple hair, who told me they were closing up the yard. As I was pulling myself together, I learned his name was Lars, and that he worked at the hostel. After seeing that I had a guitar, he asked me a few questions about what kind of music I played and offered to take me around town the next day after he finished work. Happy to have a local as a guide, we made a plan to meet up.

Back inside the café, I found a Polish girl passed out on the floor. I learned that this usually happened with people who came from the Eastern Bloc countries where weed was in short supply. After her friends carried her outside, I smoked another joint and decided to call it a night myself. When I got inside, I found someone sleeping in my bunk, so I laid down in another spot and tried to get comfortable. The whole scene felt like a combination of dorm room and unsupervised summer camp, and some of the kids were getting pretty wild. Fortunately, I wasn't as cranky then as I am now. To shut out the noise of all the people fucking around me, I put some *Ziggy Stardust* on my Walkman and eventually closed my eyes and fell asleep.

***

The next day, I woke up to discover my Walkman and Bowie cassette were gone. As I was looking around for them, some guy with a Cockney accent asked me if I'd lost something. "Fucking Gypsies! Stole the shoes right off me bloody plates," he said, while pointing to his dirty-sock-covered feet. I shrugged and was glad to still have my boots, and even more thankful that I had decided to leave my guitar at the front desk.

After taking a quick shower in a filthy stall, I headed out to the famed Green House, where I'd read some of the Cannabis Cup winners could be found. I was not disappointed. They had a fantastic selection, with some of the best weed I'd ever smoked. Since Amsterdam was a relatively small city, within a few hours I had a pretty good sense of how to get around, and spent the day checking out the different coffee shops and canals.

***

Later that afternoon, I went back to the hostel to find Lars. He was cleaning out some ashtrays and getting ready to close out his shift. His apron made him look especially thin and lanky, and with slightly hunched shoulders, he bounced around like a puppet on strings. Even though he was just a bit younger than me, he still had a curious optimism about everything. I soon learned that his dad worked in porn and his mother was a lesbian, and wondered if that had anything to do with him being so seemingly open-minded.

After clocking out, he brought a few pints over to the table I was sitting at, and introduced me to another employee named Maarten who looked like a teenaged Viking. He had long blond hair and was wearing a Metallica T-shirt. I wasn't sure why they were both interested in talking to me, but apparently weird musicians from America were a relatively rare commodity.

Assuming that all tourists would naturally want to see a bunch of washed-up-looking naked women sitting behind glass windows, Lars and Maarten decided to take me through the red-light district. After quickly seeing more than my eyes could handle, we walked over to a local bar, which was Maarten's regular hangout. It was a metalhead joint, and everyone in there looked exactly like Maarten. Judging by the fact that Lars looked a little out of his element, it soon became obvious that Lars and Maarten were not the types who normally associated with each other. After hearing about some rave that was supposedly happening in the middle of nowhere, Lars got excited and asked if we'd like to go. Maarten made a point to mention that he hated techno music, but said he would go if I wanted.

The raver scene was normally not my bag either, but since my girlfriend was part of the Global Groove collective in New York, I'd been to a bunch of the Liquid Sky and NASA parties at all the big clubs—Limelight, Shelter, Tunnel, and Club USA—even impromptu ones held in subway stations—but I had never been to one that was happening outdoors. At the very least, I expected that it would probably have some good drugs.

***

We left the bar and walked until we hit a highway, where we hitched a ride on a small truck with some guy who was in the tulip business. He was old and only spoke Dutch, but seemed more than happy to help out three weird-looking kids who were stoned out of their minds. I didn't know what the hell he was talking about with Lars and Maarten, but eventually he pulled over to the side of the road and let us out in a place that seemed to be in the middle of nowhere.

The whole area was some kind of industrial wasteland, with huge factories and smokestacks in the distance. We were on a street called Latexstraat, where I assumed they manufactured latex. We walked a little farther down the road to where it connected with Polyurethanestraat, or something like that—but no matter which way you looked, there were no signs of life. Not a tree, not a house, not a car. Nothing. As if guided by some internal compass, Lars suddenly stepped away from the road and started walking in the direction that seemed most likely to be void of any kind of civilization. By now it was so dark that we could barely see ten feet in front of us. I asked him if he knew where he was going and he said, "No, but I think this is the right way."

We kept walking for a while longer, until I started to wonder how anyone was supposed to find this place. It was obvious that whoever was throwing the party didn't want to be found easily, but this was crazy. I was starting to doubt there even was a rave, but then we all heard something in the distance. *Duum dum dum dum...* We started to pick up the pace, walking faster in the direction of the sound, and with each step closer, it got louder. It was the unmistakable repetitive beat of techno music. Most of Amsterdam is below sea level, and extremely flat. To be able to hear music before seeing where it came from meant that they were blasting that shit.

I had long hair, tattoos, and wore a septum ring, but wasn't exactly the same breed of "rocker" as Maarten, with his *Master of Puppets* T-shirt. As much as I loved me some old Metallica, I was a little more diverse in my musical sensibilities. While some of the stuff I did may have been considered a little grungy, I also dug a bunch of jazz, funk, and fusion...stuff that wasn't exactly part of Maarten's lexicon. Ultimately, I felt like rock had lost a lot of the danger it possessed back in its early days, during the mid-fifties and late sixties. And while I could appreciate the energy of some of the electronic stuff that was being made in the early nineties, I usually wouldn't go out of my way to listen to it, and generally wasn't a big fan of the club scene. I never really could get into the massive light and laser productions or the million-dollar sound systems. The crowds were always jam-packed with over-the-top trannies, club kids, and glamorous people all dolled up to the nines—and I was none of those things. To top it off, I didn't dance.

When the rave finally came into view, it was something else entirely. It looked like some kind of neo-primitive tribal pow wow. There were hundreds of half-naked people, jumping around fires and putting on displays of ritualized chaos. Since there was no access to electrical outlets, the only power came from a huge gasoline generator that supplied juice to a pair of turntables, an amp, and a handful of gigantic speakers. This was pure Rock-and-Roll. None of that corporate Pepsi-sponsored twenty-fifth-anniversary Woodstock shit going on at the same time back in upstate New York. This was different...this was some Burning Man shit.

***

A ways from where the music was being spun, there was a little trailer setup that everyone seemed to be visiting. I went inside and people were lined up behind what looked like a makeshift bar. When Lars, Maarten, and I made it up to the counter, a beautiful Nordic-looking blond chick said something I didn't understand. When I told her I didn't speak Dutch, she asked me in English what I'd like. Since I didn't see any booze, I asked her what they had. The options were Ecstasy or LSD. I asked if I could have some of both, and was given a pill and a bottle of water. After taking the pill, she told me to open my mouth, and dropped a tab of acid on my tongue. Maarten looked at me like I was crazy, and Lars was giggling and grinning, and bouncing up and down. He asked, "You took both, really?" and then he did the same. Marten mentioned that he had never tripped before and asked me what he should do. I shrugged, and the Nordic chick handed Maarten a tab. Somewhat reluctantly, he put it in his mouth. I asked the girl what I owed her and she said something about "not being able to put a price on freedom" or some other kind of European hippie socialist bullshit, but I never argued with free drugs, so I just thanked her and went outside to let the other people in line get their medicine.

When we got back outside, we stood with our backs against the trailer watching the festivities unfold. I asked Maarten how he was doing, and he replied that he hated "this kind" of music. Since he also played guitar, I understood where he was coming from, but told him that he couldn't listen to it in the same context as traditional instrument-based music. Lars, on the other hand, was bopping his head around with a big grin on his face. He asked if I was going to dance and I told him no, but that he should go ahead. A minute later, he looked at me again until I finally had to say "Go!" and he was off.

The night was getting pretty cold and I was having a hard time staying warm. A short while later, I started feeling the effects of the acid and E kicking in, and smoked a joint with Maarten. He asked me if I thought Lars might be gay, and I assured him that even if he was, he didn't have to worry 'cuz he wasn't Lars's type. A few minutes later, Lars ran back up and asked me how I was feeling, and I told him I was fine—then asked him the same question.

"This is awesome!" was all he kept saying, then he hopped back off again.

I was starting to trip and for the most part was feeling pretty good. The only problem was that I was freezing, and couldn't keep from shivering to the point that my body was shaking uncontrollably. Maarten was going on about something…probably something about how much the music sucked, but I was having a hard time paying attention. Eventually I couldn't take it anymore, so I just stopped fighting and gave in.

I told him I was going by one of the fires to warm up, and he looked at me confused, as if I was betraying some kind of guitar players' code—like he knew what I was about to do, even before I did. All I knew then was that I was cold and the fire was communicating with me…calling out to me to come near. Normally I would just sit around, watching and observing the scene, but I just couldn't stay still any longer. I walked over to one of the fires, but with people jumping around it, there was no way to get close without getting in their way. Regardless of what I might have been thinking about, or how I might have looked, my body wanted to move. I was watching my knees shake from the cold, and suddenly I just tuned in to the music and began shivering in sync with the beat. It wasn't a conscious decision. All I knew was that suddenly I was jumping around the fire…dancing. I never even thought about it. I just surrendered.

Now, even though the dancing thing was new for me, I was certainly no virgin to psychedelics. I'd had more than my fair share of hallucinogens, but up until that point, I usually had heavy mental trips where I would flirt with concepts that most people would consider borderline psychotic. It was typical for me to get caught up in some kind of craziness about the nature of God, and the universe, and all that kind of shit—but this was the first time that I was not thinking at all. I became part of a group consciousness. I was not hung up on myself as an individual and, unfortunately for Maarten, I couldn't focus on any other person either. I wasn't in that kind of head space. I was out there, in some kind of a cosmic trance.

***

Next thing I knew, the sun was coming up and I realized that I was barefoot and shirtless. I saw

Lars by another fire about thirty to forty feet away and when I ran over to him, I could see that he was pretty out there too. It took him a moment to notice me, but when he finally did, he paused to give me a big hug. Then again, he said, "This is awesome!" and went right back to dancing.

I didn't know what had happened, but ten to twelve hours had gone by in what felt like a minute. I didn't remember anything after walking over to the fire, although I too was now half-naked and covered in sweat. I knew that I had been dancing around the fire the whole night, but wasn't tired at all. I felt reborn. I know that people who don't believe in outer-body experiences won't believe it, but it happened. And it *was* awesome.

I found Maarten exactly where I'd left him, many hours earlier. "Hey Maarten! How you doin' man?" I asked. He mumbled something about how they had been playing the same song nonstop all night, but I could tell he was okay. While he was definitely in a different place, I think he had a good experience. He said he didn't understand how I had been dancing the whole time—and I told him I didn't either, that I'd just been trying to stay warm. There was simply no way to explain it. Not long after, everyone was ready to go, so I found my shoes in a pile of clothing by the fire, and we all split.

Nobody was ready to head back to town, so we found someone to hitch a ride with over to a field where Lars claimed gnomes lived. At first I thought he was joking, but he was dead serious. Anyway, what did I care about gnomes? I just wanted to find a place to chill out, get away from all the noise, and hopefully fall asleep. When we were dropped off on the side of the road, we once again had to hike it a bit—but this time Lars knew exactly where he was going. He claimed to visit the spot as often as he could. When we finally got there, I saw a big wooden pyramid set up in the middle of the field. There were also some brightly painted rocks on the ground and some other hippie-type arts-and-crafts shit scattered about. Even though there was no one around, I could tell that it was used as some kind of meeting place for weird people—which made sense because Lars was about as weird as they came. He then told Maarten and me all about the little "kabouters" who lived in that spot, and how people would come to bring them gifts. He said that once he had even been lucky enough to see one. Maarten and I laughed it off and tried to find a spot to get comfortable. We were all coming down pretty hard, and just wanted to get some rest. Within a few minutes, both Lars and Maarten were fast asleep.

I walked around for a few more minutes, trying to wind myself down, and eventually laid down inside the pyramid. I wasn't high anymore and hoping I would pass out quickly. But just as I was starting to close my eyes, I heard a high-pitched voice. At first, I thought someone was trying to play a joke, but no one was around. I looked over at Lars and Maarten and they were still sleeping. I closed my eyes again, but this time there was no

mistaking it. Someone, or something, was talking to me. There were multiple voices, speaking in a language I didn't recognize but somehow was able to understand. The voices told me that they had been waiting for me. That the time had come, and that I could not forget my mission. It was all up to me, they said…I had to save the world. As I slowly opened my eyes for the last time, I noticed that there was a bunch of little people standing all around me.

Mother…fucking…hell…

I didn't know what was happening. I knew I wasn't tripping, and even when I was, things like this rarely happened. I thought about the last time I had heard this message, during the angel-dust debacle ten years earlier, and figured I must really be going crazy this time. It was the only explanation. I jumped up and started yelling the first word that came into my mind. It was a word that I had heard in an *Animaniacs* cartoon that I guess had always been stuck in my head.

"Freunlaven. FreunLAVEN! FREUNLAVEN!!"

Lars and Maarten woke up and came running over. Maarten asked me what was wrong, but I said I didn't know. I told them that I thought maybe I was losing my mind.

Lars looked at me knowingly and said, "You saw *them*, didn't you?"

I replied, "Saw who, Lars? What the hell are you talking about? I didn't see anything!" He then asked me why I was screaming "freunlaven," but I said I didn't know…that it was just a made-up nonsense word. Both of them began shaking their heads in disbelief, and knowing I didn't speak a word of Dutch, they told me it meant FOR LIFE!

We hung out at the gnome field for a while longer, until I managed to get a grip on myself, and then headed back into town. Maarten's house was right across the street from the Melkweg and he asked if I'd like to get some rest there, since everyone would be awake at the hostel. I told him that would be great, but when I got inside, his mother took one look at me and was having none of it. She smiled politely, then called Maarten into another room and whispered something to him in Dutch. This time it wasn't all that mysterious though: she wanted me out of their fucking house, and I couldn't blame her.

Not only did I have to get out of Maarten's house, I had to get out of Holland. I needed to start thinking straight so I could figure some shit out. I walked back over to the Melkweg and bought ten grams of hashish. Then I grabbed one of the condoms from a little basket by the front desk, walked into an empty stall in the bathroom, used the rubber to wrap up the hash…and shoved it up my ass.

Then I bid my farewells to my new friends and caught a train to London.

VERMONT

S ometime around 1995, I started to hang out with my dad again. He had recently split up with my mother and somehow that resulted in us becoming closer than we had been in years. It was during this same period that we first started smoking weed together, and since I'd been out on my own for a few years by then, it seemed like he was finally starting to see me as more of an adult than a kid. I even felt confident enough to ask him if I could use his house up in Vermont, and apparently he trusted me enough to say yes.

The idea was to go on a "ski trip" with my girlfriend and another couple, Terrence and Monica, that we were friends with. I had gone on one of these ski trips a few years earlier, and that one had ended with a kid getting locked in a closet after having a psychotic reaction to LSD. Everyone became so concerned after he'd started growling and smashing cookies into his face, that in the interest of group safety it was decided that the best thing we could do was put him in a "time out." Needless to say, I was hoping this ski trip would turn out better.

The house was in a town called Arlington, and everything about it was quintessential New England. The main reason my father had purchased the house ten or so years earlier was because of its proximity to the Battenkill River. My old man was an avid fly fisherman, and since the river ran right through the backyard, and was renowned for its trout, it was an ideal location. It was a small house, situated on a half dozen acres that were originally part of a farm. There was still an old barn on the property and a sugar shack that the original owners had used to make maple syrup. It was just down the road from the house that Norman Rockwell used to live in, and there was an old white-steepled church and even a red-covered bridge nearby, all surrounded by Vermont's famous Green Mountains. The place was so idyllic that pictures of the area were even featured on postcards. It had been a few years since I'd been up to the house, but after spending weekends and summers there as a kid, I knew the place inside and out.

We left New York in the afternoon, and planned to stay at the house for a few days. Terrence and Monica were on some kind of winter break from school and wanted to go snowboarding at a ski resort called Bromley that wasn't too far away. My main objective for the trip was to try and reach a psychedelic state that would shed light on some of the questions that had recently resurfaced in Holland, and that I'd been wrestling with since leaving Europe. After that day in the gnome field, I had become obsessed. Everything had taken on a profound sense of urgency, and I was looking for answers anywhere I could find them. I thought the only way to get the information I needed was to take a dose of psilocybin larger than I ever had before. I hoped that if I could reach deep enough into my mind, everything would become clear. I thought the seclusion of the house would make it the perfect environment to push the limits, and somehow figure out what the angels and gnomes were talking about. I needed a revelation, and I thought the best way to achieve this would be to trip my balls off.

***

It was already dark when we arrived. There was snow on the ground, and the house was cold. The thermostat was always kept just warm enough to keep the pipes from freezing, and since no one had been there for a while, I got a fire going and we settled in.

I had brought more than enough weed, mushrooms, and opium to last the weekend, and wasn't looking to waste any time. I quickly measured out a standard dose of psilocybin, about 1.5 grams, for Terrence, Monica, and Karina. Since I had brought about a half-ounce, that left almost ten grams. I knew a standard dose would only produce standard results, so I decided to step it up a bit. I was originally planning on taking about five or six grams, but at the last moment said *fuck it* and decided to take it all. There was no point in pussyfooting around—I was on a mission. We each had a cup of boiling water to steep our mushrooms, and we added a little lavender and honey to sweeten the fungal brew.

It was probably about 10:00 p.m. when we finally drank down the psilocybin tea. I immediately felt the strange queasy feeling in my stomach, a familiar side effect of the drug; the combination of the mushrooms and the anticipation almost always brought it on. I knew it was going to be a heavy trip, and was glad there wasn't anything that could interrupt it. After about twenty minutes, I could feel my sense of awareness becoming heightened, in a way where sounds and colors seemed to be communicating with me in a mutual state of clairvoyance. We were listening to the Tony Williams Lifetime album *Emergency*, which I knew had the potential to make things get really weird, so I decided to change it to something that would be a little more conducive to maintaining the vibe. The reason I remember this is because I wound up putting on *You* by Gong, which changed the mood drastically after only the first few bars. The music was all about gnomes, which, coincidentally, I got turned on to by some musicians in London right after I left Holland. I don't know how much time passed after the CD started, but I was beginning to trip out and was getting really horny.

I went upstairs with my woman and we started

to do what couples do. Gong was doing that sexy psychedelic witch funk that they do, and all of my senses were going into overdrive. I could feel the blood coursing through my veins. All the visual, aural, emotional, sensual, and cerebral centers of my mind and body were starting to transcend the realms of time and space. I was pumping in and out of Karina's wet pussy and all of my chakras were starting to align. I had found the groove and was heading toward the light. I was so close! But just as I was about to lay down all thoughts and surrender to the void, I heard a phone ring.

At first I thought the universe was calling me and all I had to do was pick up the phone for the secrets to be revealed. But it just kept ringing and ringing...

This was before everyone and their mother had a cell phone. Before Twitter, and Facebook, and all that social-networking bullshit that has turned everyone's lives into a never-ending stream of continuous communication. But eventually I realized this was not a call from the cosmos—this was the ring of an actual phone. And it rang, and it rang.

I wasn't expecting any calls because nobody knew we were there. No one ever called there. Hell, I didn't think anyone even knew the number. This was the place where you went when you didn't want to be bothered. It was so rare for a phone to ring there that it took me a minute to remember there even *was* a phone. But then I remembered the old rotary job—with an actual bell that would ring—downstairs in the living room. And it was still ringing!

I couldn't take it anymore. My whole high was getting totally fucked up! Just as I was about to lose my goddamned mind, I finally yelled down the stairs:

"SOMEBODY PICK UP THE FUCKING PHONE!"

Terrence, who was downstairs, doing God knows what, eventually picked it up. "Hello? …What?" I was more tuned in to that conversation than any other in my entire life. I couldn't hear what was being said on the other end of the line, but knew that Terrence was totally fucked up too. I just kept hearing him repeat, "Um…I don't know"—pause—"I don't know," until he called up to me and asked, "Hey Davy! Who are we?"

Who are we? I wondered. *What does that even mean? …Who* really *are any of us?*

"Are we owners, or the renters?"

I wasn't sure what the hell he was talking about, but I yelled back down to him, "We're the owners!"

And then Terrence got back on the phone and said, "We are the owners." Then said "okay" and hung up.

I ran downstairs with my dick hanging out, and began the inquisition, "Who the FUCK was that?"

"I don't know," Terrence said. "I think the community."

The *community*, I'm thinking? *Who the hell is the community? What the fuck is he talking about?*

"Well, what did they want?" I asked.

"They were taking a survey," he said. "They wanted to know if we were the owners or if we were renting."

My mind started racing. I knew it was too late for a survey, and I started breaking down every possible scenario for what was *going on*. The thing about hallucinogens is you can think of and explore a million different possibilities simultaneously, but once you become paranoid and focus on one thing, it's all over. Within a minute, I knew exactly what was "*going on*"...

There weren't many neighbors nearby...but there were some. The closest was a few hundred yards away, but close enough to see that someone was in the house. I decided one of the neighbors must have seen a couple of weird-looking kids show up. The lights were on late and they might have heard strange music being played very loudly. They hadn't seen me around for years, and even if they had, I wouldn't have looked how they remembered. The house was empty most of the time...and when someone was there it was my dad, who they knew...with his canoe and bird whistles and shit. One time, some local kids broke in and partied a bit. Nothing was stolen...they just drank some beer and messed the place up a little. My dad probably asked the neighbors if they could keep an eye on the house when he was gone. They were doing the right thing. They see some strange-looking kids show up at the house one night... They don't recognize the car... *Of course* they would call to see if everything is all right. But then they speak to some kid who is obviously totally fucked up and who doesn't even know whose house it is?

I added it all up in my head…

Since it was my house, everyone was looking to me to know what I was thinking. They didn't know anything was wrong, except they saw me looking crazy and deep in thought. When someone finally asked me what was happening, I told them: "THEY ARE CALLING THE POLICE, AND WE ARE GOING TO JAIL!"

It all made perfect sense… But, of course, I was on almost ten grams of mushrooms and was completely out of my mind. I knew I couldn't freak out. Part of the reason I was taking them in the first place was to overcome my fears, to learn to control my mind, to become a psychedelic warrior! I needed to try and think… What would Castaneda's Don Juan do?

I looked down and saw these weird white branches growing in a million crazy directions right in front of me. What are *those*, I wondered. Oh yeah…they are my *fucking hands!* Everyone was looking at me. I needed discipline…I needed to figure this shit out!

So I decided it must be one of the neighbors…but which one? Could I find them in time and stop them from calling the police? Would I have to kill them? Hopefully not…Surely it was too late for that anyway. I didn't know where the police would be coming from, but knew there were only two ways to get to the house…and either way they would need to cross a bridge. Maybe the neighbors hadn't called the police yet... Maybe they were watching to see what we would do first...

There was a small telescope and a pair of binoculars by the window. I grabbed them and started looking out into the night... I stared down the road, in the direction of the nearest bridge...the one that I figured they would most likely be coming from. Nothing was happening. I didn't know how much time had passed, or how much time we had left, but the suspense was killing me... Where were they?

Finally, I saw a car crossing the bridge about a half mile down the road... It turned toward the house and then just stopped. I couldn't see what was going on. The car looked like it was parked by another house down the road, but its headlights were pointed in our direction...maybe the people who called *them*. What were they doing... What were they waiting for?? Surely they must be spying back at us to see if they needed to call in reinforcements. Who could blame them... *They* didn't know who we were. Maybe we were a cult and were armed to the teeth! They were probably sending in a SWAT team to survey the situation. Maybe it would turn out like the Branch Davidian compound in Waco... I hoped they wouldn't just burn us down... I figured they didn't need any more bad publicity. And then suddenly it looked like a spotlight was turned on. I told Terrence to turn out the lights. I wasn't going to make this any easier for them. After a minute of sitting in the dark, the girls got nervous and said they wanted the lights back on. Good idea. They probably had night-vision goggles and heat-seeking technology anyway.

What was *taking* them so long? Maybe they were running the plates on the car to see who we were. Would they call first to negotiate our surrender, or just crash in through the windows on ropes lowered from the roof? If they saw the plates, they would know we were from New York. *Everybody* hates people from New York. We were trapped. God, why didn't they just get it over with already??

And then I had an even worse thought: they knew exactly who I was, and they knew all about my mission! They knew I was just about to get my instructions so they decided they had to sabotage me. They had to stop me before I could find out how to save the world!! Were government officials working as henchmen for the forces of evil? Or was this some group of independent assassins who had pledged their allegiance to the dark one? I just wasn't sure...

I didn't know what to do. The standoff had been going on for too long, and I wasn't yet trained for this kind of warfare. I was failing my test as a psychic shaman, and I knew it. I couldn't take them on all alone... I needed help... I needed someone strong and wise. I really didn't want to do it. I knew he would be pissed off, but decided I had no choice. I was going to call my dad.

I took a few minutes to build up the nerve.

Joseph Davida

He'd just recently started to treat me like an adult, and here I was about to tell him…what exactly? Maybe he could call the bastards off and we could end this peacefully. To try and pull myself together, I took a hit of weed, but knew instantly it was a bad idea… Fractals were breaking up everywhere, and I was hitting my peak. I dialed the phone.

"Hello?"

Thank God. He sounded like he was awake. "Dad?"

"Hey, are you up at the house?"

"Yeah."

"Did you make it up there all right in the snow?"

"Yeah."

"Good, good. Well, what's going on?"

"Dad, I'm tripping my brains out, the police are coming, and I'm going to jail!"

"*What?* What are you talking about?"

I told him everything that was *happening*, until he finally cut me off: "You are allowed to be at that house! It is my house, and you are my son. It is *your* house."

"But, Dad, I have a big bag of weed, and mushrooms, and…" (I think I left out the opium.) "Should I throw everything in the fire?"

"What? No, no, don't throw it in the fire! Just go put it all upstairs and, if the cops come by, just tell them who you are! Everything will be fine. If there is any problem, just call me back."

I got off the phone feeling a lot better. My father was the fucking man. How come I didn't think of any of that? Of *course* I was allowed to be in the house. There were pictures of me on the wall for Christ's sake! I had every right to be there. I was *supposed* to be there. Those fucking Gestapo pigs couldn't come down on me!

I was still a little nervous about the impending confrontation, but was definitely starting to feel a lot more confident. I hid the drugs in a vanity table upstairs, and then looked at myself in the mirror. Oh no. Bad idea... Don't *ever* look in the mirror when you're tripping your face off. Next I went over to the window and looked back down the road. They were still there. At least an hour must have passed and they were *still* just sitting there. I stood watching them, until I finally saw them start to move toward the house. "All right, everyone. Be cool! I will just answer the door and tell them this is my dad's house. We are on a ski trip, and we are allowed to be here."

I was still watching through the binoculars as they slowly came down the road toward the house. As they got closer, I realized that they were actually in a truck...with a big tank on the back? When it finally got close enough that I could see it with my own eyes, I noticed there were words painted on the side of the tank: *Tom's Emergency Plumbing Service + Septic Repair.* Then they just passed right on by the house and kept driving.

"What happened?" asked Terrence, who was crouching behind the couch, as if preparing for a shootout. I didn't know. Suddenly I realized that nothing was happening. Maybe nothing had ever been happening. A half hour earlier, I'd been ready for battle, but now I realized that the battle was all in my mind. How was I supposed to save the world? I couldn't even save myself! Hell, I started to wonder if there even *was* anything to save? I certainly was no psychedelic warrior. I was a fucking paranoid idiot. Everyone was looking at me with confused expressions, trying to figure out what the fuck was going on. I'd not only fucked up my own trip, but everyone else's as well. I had failed my test.

The rest of the trip passed without incident, and the only real danger we were ever in was when we were too stoned to navigate the ski lifts. All of that insanity because of a phone call. If I was able to create all of that, surely I must have created the rest of the apocalyptic craziness as well. I tried not to make a big deal out of everything that had happened, but I was embarrassed and depressed. Once again, I had to hand it to my old man for saving my ass. To say thanks, I left a big bud of the Chronic for him in his drawer so he'd have something good to smoke the next time he went up to the house.

Just as we were packing up and getting ready to leave, I found a note by the phone. It said, *Talk to the professor.* I didn't think much of it at first, figuring it had something to do with someone's schoolwork—but on the drive back to New York, I asked Terrence and Monica about it out of mild curiosity. They insisted they didn't know what I was talking about though, and while I couldn't think of who else would have written it, or where it could have come from, I decided to just forget about it.

NEPAL

In the spring of 1997, all of my worst fears were confirmed. The paranoia that I normally considered a mainly self-induced side effect of psychotropic drugs began to manifest itself in a very sobering way. Shit was starting to get very real. Even though I had decided to lay off the psychedelics for a little while after the Vermont trip, my best friend asked if I could get him a pound of mushrooms for a deal he had lined up on Long Island. I regularly sold large quantities of weed, but hallucinogens were a whole different bag. The problem was they were in a different class of drugs than weed, and apparently you could somehow be charged with attempting to overthrow the government. Regardless, Jerry convinced me that it was cool, and that he knew what he was doing. Somewhat reluctantly, I relented, contacted my connection, and picked up the pound for him.

The next day, I got a phone call from Jerry. He had been arrested and was facing some pretty serious charges. The guy he had done the deal with turned out to be a snitch and the whole thing was a setup. As soon as Jerry handed over the bag and took the cash, the place lit up like the Fourth of July with police cars that had been waiting for the transaction to go down. After being arrested, the police told him they could work out some kind of deal with him, so long as he ratted out *his* connection...who essentially was me.

I had known Jerry since we were kids, and knew he would never intentionally give me up, but when someone is facing a few years in jail, it's hard to know for sure what they are really thinking. Even though I knew I wouldn't be lining up new deals with him any time soon, I was still conducting plenty of other business that could have resulted in me sharing a similar fate. It started to feel like the dark forces of the psychic Gestapo could really be closing in this time, and I knew I had to find someone who could help me. I figured if I didn't yet have the training to safely navigate my own world, how would I ever be able to save everyone else's? I needed to find a guru.

In the mid-nineties, all things Eastern were trending pretty hard, and I have to admit that I too was sufficiently guilty. I had spent a few years reading books on Eastern philosophy and religion, and I was pretty well entranced. I had a copy of the *Tibetan Book of the Dead* that I had repeatedly tried to digest, but like most of what I had read from that part of the world, I really couldn't figure out how to apply any of it. The idea of reaching an enlightened state—without drugs—sounded great on paper, but I didn't actually know anyone who was enlightened. Since Tibet was inaccessible at the time, I decided my best bet was Nepal. Not only had many Tibetan monks fled to Nepal as refugees, but a bunch of Hindu mystics were living there as well. I couldn't waste any more time; I had to find some answers. Not being one for extensive planning, I found a travel agent in the trusty *Village Voice* and bought two roundtrip tickets for me and Karina to Kathmandu. As soon as I held the tickets in my hand, I immediately felt a sense of empowerment. It was time for my pilgrimage.

***

I'd tried to get everything in order before the flight was scheduled to leave, but somehow by the time me and the woman finally jumped in a cab to head to the airport, we were already running pretty late. Naturally there was a ton of traffic on the BQE, but I figured enlightened beings couldn't be bothered with such things ahead of time. Inevitably, me and the woman started arguing about whose fault it was, and it was starting to look like we might miss the flight altogether. By the time we got to the terminal, stress levels were peaking and tensions were running high. JFK was not turning out to be the most conducive starting point for a spiritual journey…and we were literally running through the airport, trying to make it to the gate in time. They were already in the process of boarding and the flight had apparently been overbooked. But we knew they couldn't possibly tell us that we were too late—surely they knew that people flying to Kathmandu had to be special, right?

But of course, we were not flying directly into Nepal…on a plane filled with other special people…on their own spiritual journeys to visit the birthplace of Siddhartha. We were flying Pakistani Air, with a layover in Karachi.

Somehow we managed to get on the plane, but right away knew that it was not going to be some enchanted voyage. For starters, the flight was almost twenty-four hours long, and at six foot three, *any* flight in coach was a daunting prospect. And this was going to be the longest flight I'd ever been on. We were seated in the middle row, shoulder to shoulder with sweaty men and burka-clad women. I initially thought the fact that I'd be able to smoke was a good thing, but after an hour it was already getting difficult to breathe. The air became so dry and stale, I was constantly running to the bathroom to snort water up my nose in a futile attempt to keep my nasal passages moist.

Living in Manhattan, I was used to being surrounded by people of different cultures, but these were the closest quarters I'd ever had to actually share with one of them. Despite the man next to me's continuous effort to cuddle—by putting his head on my shoulder, while simultaneously managing to sleep, fart, and pick his nose—it was impossible to find a comfortable position. It was even difficult to get up and stretch because the aisles were filled with men calculating the direction of Mecca to perform their daily prayers. Every few hours, the flight attendants served a different variation of curry. While I already wasn't a huge fan of the stuff, the mass-produced variety just seemed to reinforce my dislike of it.

Unlike the people who were happy to prostrate themselves in prayer on the floor of a twenty-five-year-old 747, I realized I was not yet a spiritual being. The woman and I were blaming each other for our respective misery in a series of snarls, growls, and showings of teeth—and after fifteen hours, I felt like a caged animal, ready to commit some horrible crime. Five or six salats later, we finally landed in Karachi.

***

During the layover, we saw a crowd of people gathered around one of the small TVs that was set up in the terminal. They were watching WWF wrestling and were *ooohing* and *aaahing* every time one of the wrestlers got "hurt." I wasn't in the mood to watch men in tights throw one another around a ring; I was tired and sore, and ready to cut off a limb for the chance to take a shower and go to bed. I knew the flight to Kathmandu would not be nearly as long as the first leg, but as much as we just wanted to "get there already," we were both dreading the idea of having to get back on a plane for another three hours. Although when the time finally came to board the next flight, we were more than ready to escape the purgatory that was the waiting room of the Karachi airport.

We quickly discovered that our new plane was much smaller than the one we left New York on, and there were a lot less people going to our final destination. Not long after taking off, it also became apparent that the cabin was not properly pressurized, making my ears feel like they could start bleeding at any moment. This was exacerbated by the fact that there were live chickens on the plane that seemed to become especially frenzied every time we hit some heavy turbulence. By the time we hit the ground, our nerves were totally frayed and I was afraid we might kill each other before we got off the plane.

I was one of the only Westerners on the plane and, along with my Korean girlfriend, we must have looked like a strange couple. Exhausted, nauseous, and agitated, we were practically screaming at each other as we waited for someone to open the doors, and I could tell we were making the other passengers nervous. Fortunately, there was no waiting to taxi into a gate because there were no gates. I looked out the window and could see only one small terminal. We were parked in the middle of the landing strip and there were no other planes in sight. After a few minutes, someone pushed a small set of portable stairs up to the plane, and the doors opened. Despite the fact that we had lost all notions of spirituality, let alone any semblance of mere humanity, something amazing happened.

The second we stepped off the plane, we were both immediately silenced by a tremendous invisible force. It was like being bitch-slapped in the face by the right hand of God. I knew the woman felt it too because when I looked over at her, she looked like she was in awe. The second I took my first breath, I instantly felt an incredible burst of energy.

***

After we got our visas and cleared customs, we walked outside the terminal and found a few taxis lined up by the doors. The drivers were trying to hustle us over to whatever lodging establishment they received a commission from, but when I announced that I wanted to go to the Kathmandu Guesthouse, a small man ran up and hurried us into one of the tiny cabs. Not long after we started heading down the one-lane Nepalese highway, we saw small farms with fields being plowed by oxen. The countryside was immense, vast, and beautiful.

We came to a stop in the middle of the road, but before I could ask the driver why we were stopping, I saw a brace of ducklings crossing the road behind their mother. The woman and I, who had hardly said a word to each other since landing, just looked at each other in bewilderment. It took everything we had to keep from laughing hysterically. We didn't need to say it, but we both knew that if we had to turn around and head back to the airport at that minute, the trip would have been worth it. A day and a half earlier, we were in another taxi, willing to kill anything in our way to get through traffic as quickly as possible—but somehow there in Nepal, it quickly dawned on us that we weren't shit. Just another small part of the enormous interconnected web of life.

That car ride to the Guesthouse was my first real glimpse of the East. It was my first time in a place that still seemed to maintain some kind of balance with nature, and my first time in a country without a McDonalds...and somehow, that meant something. When we finally made it into Kathmandu, my faith in humanity had already been restored.

There was a long gated driveway leading up to the little hotel, and when we stepped out of the car, we were greeted by a staff member with a warm "Namaste!" There was a group of trekkers who had just returned from climbing Everest in the lobby, and right after we checked in, we were shown into a simple, but clean, little room. Despite the lack of sleep and accumulated grime of two days' worth of traveling, we were dying to get out and explore. We dropped off our bags and hit the streets.

Immediately after exiting the hotel, a rickshaw driver rode up beside us. "Hello, sir! Where do you come from? America? Oh, USA is *very* good. Wherever you would like to go sir, I can take you!" He told us his name was Casey, but after a minute I realized he was actually saying K.C., which I assumed was derived from the fact that he was wearing an old Kansas City Royals hat. As we walked, he drove alongside us and continued to ask various questions.

At first, I felt embarrassed at the idea of having a guy, who couldn't have weighed a hundred pounds soaking wet, pedaling us around on an antique bicycle. It had no gears and looked to be eighty years old…but he was very persistent about his trade. After a few minutes, I figured I could trust him and asked him the big question that was on my mind: "K.C., there is one thing you might be able to help me with—do you know where I can get some hashish?"

He sat up a little straighter on his bike, looked over both his shoulders, and whispered back, "Yes sir, I know."

I asked him if it was safe.

"Yes sir, it's okay."

I said, "Okay then. Take me there." At once, my resistance to becoming the ugly American was outweighed by my urge to get stoned.

The minute we got into that rickshaw, any ideas I had about cultural assimilation went out the window. The reality that I was a foreigner with money was apparent. Once K.C. began to pedal, I started wrestling with the ethical question of whether it was wrong to have him pull us around like some "coolie"—or worse, not let him do his job and rob him of the chance to make some money for his family. I didn't yet know. In New York, I was used to being at the lower end of the financial ladder, but in Nepal I was suddenly at the top of a class structure that was thousands of years old. None of my utopian ideals could change that.

Despite not yet knowing my place in this strange new world, I decided that so long as I could get the hash problem resolved on the first day, I would be able to figure the rest out later, and get on with what I had originally set out to do in Nepal. The problem with the hash, of course, was that I didn't have any—and the one thing that I *did* know was that there was no way the mission could start without it.

K.C. started pedaling us down these little ancient-looking back streets, until we arrived at a small building down an alley. He then jumped off the rickshaw and told us to wait as he knocked on a door. He went inside, then came out a few minutes later and asked, "Black or white?" I told him I didn't know, and asked if I could see it—but he looked a little nervous, and I didn't want to make things more difficult for him, so I said black. He told me it would be 4,000 rupees, and although I normally wasn't in the business of handing over money without getting something immediately in return, I realized I didn't have much choice. Despite not knowing the going rate for a rickshaw, I figured the worst that could happen was I'd wind up with a really cool oversized souvenir. I didn't know how much, or even what I was supposed to be getting, but I decided to trust him, and handed him the money.

He wound up running down some little alley,

and after a few minutes I started to figure I'd been beat. I decided if they wouldn't let me take the rickshaw back home on the plane, I could always ride alongside some other tourists and yell out: "Hello sir! Where are you from?" in an attempt to recoup my losses. Just as we began wondering if we should just ditch the rickshaw and split before we wound up in a Nepalese prison, K.C. came running up and hopped back on the seat. When he handed me a nice big chocolate brown ball about half the size of my fist, I was ready to kiss him! It had to have been about two ounces, and at less than a dollar a gram, it was a great fucking deal! I could have sold it in New York for at least ten times that amount. I could only imagine what the white kind was. Charas? Kif? I decided not to push my luck. I had more than enough to last the whole trip, and I could tell that K.C. was relieved to have the ordeal behind him. I didn't know if he got a cut out of the deal, so I offered him a couple bucks, but he refused to take it.

Although without skipping a beat, he asked, "Where would you like me to take you now, sir?" And then I knew that he had us.

"I don't know, K.C. Where is a good place to go?"

"Well, I can take you down Freak Street, Monkey Temple, Durbar Squa—"

"Monkey Temple!" I shouted. "How much to go there?"

He said some amount that worked out to less than a dollar, so I said, "Okay K.C., take us there!"

***

On the way to the Monkey Temple, I pinched off a piece of the hash and rolled it into a thin string with my fingers. After threading it into a cigarette, I lit it up and could taste its rich flavor. K.C. was pointing out all the different sights and for the first time in my life, I felt truly happy. I wondered if it could ever get any better than this. How could I have ever questioned being beaten by him? These were special people! They were tuned into a higher frequency! And besides, I was on a mission from God! At that moment, nothing could ever go wrong...

Everywhere I looked was beauty. Even the things that weren't meant to look beautiful were beautiful. There were little statues of Buddhist and Hindu deities all over the place. Even the old worn-out ones, in little tucked-away places, were apparently revered, as evidenced by the adornment of a fresh flower or some *tika* powder. There were sacred brahman cows in the road, and the most amazing-looking people in traditional Nepalese clothing going about their routines. The sights, sounds, and smells were intoxicating, and all my senses were so overwhelmed I was almost giddy. It truly was Shangri-la.

When we finally got to the Monkey Temple, K.C. pulled over to the side of the road, where we saw an ancient stone stairwell that went the rest of the way up the mountain. On the walk up, we passed Tibetan craftspeople selling handicrafts, and not long after, we started to see the monkeys. They were just hanging out, going about normal monkey business, and you could tell they knew it was *their* temple. Although people left them food, they were essentially wild and had the run of the place. When we got to the top, the monkeys were everywhere...living throughout the entire temple. It was out of this world.

The Monkey Temple is actually the nickname for a Buddhist temple called Swayambhunath. It had a giant ornate *stupa*, and huge prayer wheels that people walked around while reciting mantras. I couldn't believe places like this actually existed— it was beyond anything I could have ever imagined. I felt high in a way that I never had before, and it definitely wasn't just the hash. There was *something* there, and it seemed to permeate everything.

On the side of the temple there was an amazing view over the city, and as I was standing there it felt like I was in some kind of a dream. I don't know if it was because I had never been anywhere even remotely like it, but my mind was blown, like the first time I'd seen *Star Wars*. After trying to put the whole scene into perspective, I walked around a corner and found a teenage girl sweeping the ground with a bunch of branches tied together as a broom—listening to a little transistor radio. Just when I felt like I had been transported somewhere completely untouched and untainted by the West, I heard Gwen Stefani singing "Don't speak..." No Happy Meals, Walmarts, or Ford F-150s, but they did have "No Doubt."

On the way down, I bought some beautiful little hand-carved statues made by the Tibetan refugees. From there, K.C. took us through Durbar Square, where we saw Kumari's temple and the most incredible stacked pagoda-shaped buildings. When we got back to the Guesthouse, I asked what I owed him, and he said some ridiculous amount that worked out to less than three dollars. When I tried to give him 1,000 rupees, he initially refused, but after a little persuasion he finally accepted and we turned in for the night.

***

On the way out for breakfast the next morning, K.C. was dutifully waiting for us by the gate. We told him we just wanted to eat and walk around Thamel a bit, but promised that as long as we were in Kathmandu we would use no other "tour guide" but him. On the corner down from the Guesthouse were little gangs of children begging and selling cigarettes. I gave a few of them some change, and as we were walking around looking for a place to eat, I noticed that the crowd was growing larger. I was out of coins and knew if I started handing out bills there was likely to be a riot—so we ducked into a café, where the proprietor shooed them away like stray dogs.

We ordered some tea, toast, eggs, and bacon and while everything was fine, the bacon turned out to be a slab of pork that was a bit heavy for the first meal of the day. I had it wrapped and gave it to some of the kids on the street, who devoured it right in front of me. With big smiles, they told me that it "was the best chicken they ever tasted!" I then realized that not only had they probably never eaten pork before, but that they possibly had never eaten chicken either.

After buying some *thankas* and singing bowls on Freak Street, as well as a few clay chillums that we put to immediate use, we met back up with K.C., who had a magical way of showing up whenever we needed him. That day, he suggested that we visit Pashupatinath, the holiest Hindu temple in Kathmandu. On the way, there were a few steep hills where I hopped out to help him push the rickshaw. It made him a little uncomfortable when I tried to help, but I just couldn't sit there and yell "Faster, boy!" as he struggled to pull our weight. When I asked him if it wasn't common for others to help, he admitted most didn't. He did say he liked Americans though, and alluded to the fact that a lot of Europeans generally treated him like shit. I think he knew upon first meeting us that we didn't subscribe to any of that caste bullshit, but he still didn't know what to make of us. The fact that we were an interracial couple probably said *something*, but more than anything, we would have fun with him and try to include him in whatever it was that we were doing. To the obvious dismay of the restaurant owners, we would even ask him to eat with us...but we didn't know the rules, and we didn't care—and I think K.C. really appreciated that. Even if some people didn't treat him like a human being, he was one of the most humble and stand-up guys I have ever met.

***

Pashupatinath had a different vibe from the Monkey Temple. The inside was technically off limits to non-Hindus, but there was a river that ran through the back of the temple complex that was considered the most holy after the Ganges. As soon as we arrived, a *sadhu* came up to me and put a tika on my forehead. I don't think he had ever seen a Westerner quite like me, and was digging the fact that I had hair down to my ass and wore a septum ring. We actually looked pretty similar, except that aside from a loin cloth, he was practically naked. To try and get past our communication barrier, I broke off a piece of hash for him. He responded with a loud "Bom Shiva!" and touched it to his forehead. Was it possible he was the one I was looking for? The one who could give me some answers and the power I needed to *save the world?* I wasn't sure yet…it was still too early to tell.

There were half-clad sadhus everywhere, sitting out on blankets, with long dreadlocks, either worn straight down or tied up in a knot on top of their heads. They all had beards and white stripes painted on their foreheads, with red dots placed in the middle to symbolize their third eye. Most wore beads around their necks and carried silver tridents and small bowls to receive alms. The majority of them also seemed to really like smoking hash. I thought if I could ever give up the pussy, I'd probably make a good sadhu myself. Maybe that was the training I needed, and wondered if that was my calling...the reason I was there.

There was a funeral taking place down by the river, and a body was burning on top of a pile of logs. Everywhere you looked, you got the sense that the cycles between life and death meant something different. There was so much out there, so much to learn, that I decided it should be mandatory for everyone to get out of their comfort zone at least once, like the Amish who take a year out of their own communities for *Rumspringa*. Everyone needed to experience something like this, and I was starting to wonder how I would ever be able to step back into my life in New York.

***

One day while talking with K.C. about what I did back home, I made some offhand comment about a song I was working on, and realized that he'd never heard of the Beatles. In my mind the Beatles were the biggest thing in the world, the pinnacle of everything I aspired to achieve. To discover that people actually could live their entire lives without ever being aware of the biggest rock band to ever exist was a shock to me. It suddenly made me realize that no matter how much of a big deal I thought I might one day become, half of the planet would go on living fulfilling, meaningful lives, and never give a shit about me, or what I considered important.

***

For the next few days, we hung out meditating at the temples, smoking chillums and getting stoned. With every passing hour I was becoming a little bit more immersed, and seriously began to consider not going home at all. One day we went over to one of the biggest Buddhist temples, called Bhodanath, which had prayer flags hanging from lines off the steeple and the iconic painted image of the Buddha's eyes. There were monks on pilgrimages, praying in their red and orange robes, and all of them seemed to know something I didn't.

Suddenly I heard a sound unlike anything I'd ever heard before. It was one long, deep note that came from an instrument that sounded like some cross between a tuba and a trumpet. The note was held for a long time and then was followed by a wild cacophony of drums and cymbals. I ran over to where the sound was coming from, and found rows of Tibetan monks sitting inside the temple. A gelupa lama in a gigantic mohawk-shaped hat was leading a procession of chants. They were all chanting in unison, making a sound so deep it was hard to comprehend it actually being produced by human beings. I suspected that maybe *they* knew the secret, but it seemed rude to try and interrupt them. The more I listened, the more I realized that maybe their chants *were* the secret.

I climbed back up by a ledge near the top of the stupa and sat down with my legs crossed and my eyes closed. I listened to the monks' chanting, and repeated their mantra with them: "OHM MANI PADME HUUUUUM!" The world seemed to disappear, and for a moment it felt like I was floating. And then I received a message, as if it was translated directly into my brain: "You must go to the jungle!"

I had K.C. take me back into town, and found a little travel agency to make arrangements to go to a place called the Chitwan Jungle Lodge. It was situated right in the middle of the Chitwan National Park, and was one of the few places left in the world that was known for having a healthy population of Bengal tigers. The travel agent found someone who could drive us to the park, and we told K.C. we would find him when we returned.

About five minutes after getting on the highway, we got behind a truck with emissions so noxious, that it was almost impossible to breathe. (USA emission standards #1!!!) The road had only one narrow lane in each direction, and there was no easy way to pass. We were driving pretty fast, winding through these mountain roads with no guardrails, but even when I tried to cover my face there was no way to avoid the smoke. We would pass a truck, only to wind up behind another a minute or two later. It was like that for hours.

When we got a bit farther west, I finally got my first glimpse of the Himalayan mountain range, and although it was some of the most beautiful terrain I had ever seen, it was difficult to appreciate because I was too busy trying not to choke.

When we arrived in Bharatpur, we got off the main road and were met by a Land Rover that was waiting to take us into the park. We started driving down a dirt path through some fields until we eventually hit a river that had to be at least fifty feet wide. Since there didn't appear to be any bridge, the driver told us to hold our bags over our heads, and drove right into the water until the floorboards were full. A minute later, we were driving through dense vine-covered trees that grew thicker and thicker, until it dawned on me that we'd finally made it to the jungle.

Eventually we pulled into a clearing where we were met by some elephants, but aside from the herd, and the people who worked in the park, we seemed to be the only ones there. After jumping out of the vehicle, we were introduced to the staff and given a tour of the lodge. One of the guides told us we were free to wander around, so long as we didn't leave the campground. Tigers could be anywhere.

***

The next morning, we woke at the crack of dawn, and met the elephant who was taking us into the jungle. Her name was Anarkali, and she was gorgeous. I gave her a few apples I had stolen at breakfast, and we hit it off right away. After kissing her trunk, rubbing her chin, and whispering sweet nothings into her ear (we were practically making out), I jumped onto her back and headed out into the bush. It was the first time I had ever seen monkeys, guar, and white rhino outside of a zoo, and it was incredible. At one point, Anarkali got a little skittish because our *manhout* told us a tiger was hiding in the grass nearby. Although we couldn't get a clear view, just knowing that it was so close, with no glass or bars between us, was exhilarating.

***

Every day when we returned from our expedition, I would go over to where the elephants lived and bring them whatever snacks I could grab from the lodge. They would get excited when they saw me coming, and I had a feeling it wasn't just for the food. It was something deeper, in a way that is hard to describe. It seemed as if they were able to look into my soul, and somehow because of this I felt determined to prove myself worthy in a way I rarely feel around other humans.

The last night there, we had a little party, and sat around a bonfire playing guitars and smoking hash with some of the employees who lived at the lodge. After a while, I snuck away and headed over to see the elephants. Most appeared to be sleeping, but I found Anarkali was still awake. She stood there in the dark playing with a branch, and seemed to be contemplating the mysteries of the universe. As I got closer to her, I saw that she had a huge shackle around one of her ankles, and realized that she lived in what basically amounted to an elephant work camp. She was essentially a slave—and although I considered trying to free her, knew that this was all she had ever known. She was related to all of the other elephants, and this was her home. This was her life.

But I could tell by the way that she was looking at me, with her big beautiful eyes, that she already understood all of this. It was at that moment that I finally realized we all have our own shackles—that life *is* suffering. It is only after we accept this that we may truly become compassionate beings, and only then that we might actually find some peace. I gave her a hug, petted her trunk, and told her I was going to miss her.

***

When we got back to Kathmandu, I picked up a snappy little Punjabi suit for myself, and bought the woman a beautiful hand-embroidered sari. After receiving some help putting it on correctly, she walked out of the dressing room looking like a Nepalese princess. We looked at ourselves in a little mirror mounted on the wall, and I think we both realized that we could be very happy staying in Nepal forever. Even though the Nepalese people probably thought we came from Mars, they were the most gracious people we had ever met.

Something had happened there, and I felt different than I ever had before. I was at peace.

As the trip was coming to a close, we started dreading the idea of having to head back to New York. I still hadn't found my guru and was no closer to carrying out my mission. I was also just about out of money, and knew if I stayed much longer, I would have to find a job—and wasn't sure I was cut out for the rickshaw life. Even though cash was in short supply, I still had a big ball of hash that, despite the temptation, I decided wasn't worth carrying back on the plane.

I had K.C. take me back over to Pashupatinath and I found the same sadhu I'd met the first day we visited the temple. I handed him the big chunk of hash, and once again he held it up to his forehead and yelled out "Bom Shiva!" Then he took out his tika powder and put a red dot on my third eye. Afterward, he reached his hand out and placed it on my shoulder, looked deep into my eyes, and started to say something. At first I thought he was just really happy that I had given him so much hash, but he continued speaking until I had to ask K.C. what he was saying. Although they spoke different dialects, K.C. tried to keep up.

"Mister Joe, sadhu say you have more work. He say this is just beginning, but! he say you are more strong now, but needing more learning still. He say now you have to go home. You need find teacher...no, no...not teacher. Find professor!"

The sadhu repeated the last word in English. "Professor!"

I didn't know what they were talking about, but the more questions I asked, the more confusing it got. They were essentially repeating the same things over and over until I was out of time. I had a flight to catch.

Before we left, we said our goodbyes to K.C. and I gave him what little money I had left. I held on to just enough cash to take a cab to the airport in Nepal, and to get back to my apartment from JFK. I didn't carry any credit cards back then and, in retrospect, leaving myself with almost no cash was very stupid. I bowed and waved one last time to K.C., and jumped in the taxi. Right before we drove off, he yelled out, "Find the professor!"

The way K.C. said it made me wonder if everything the sadhu had been telling me may have actually come from K.C himself. I had been looking for answers from holy men, monks, and sadhus, but suddenly I realized that the person who had actually taught me the most was our humble rickshaw driver. *My guide.* When it all finally hit me, I wanted to turn around. But it was too late. We were already on our way home.

***

The problems started when we landed in Pakistan. For some reason, an officer told us we had to go through customs, even though we were just trying to get to another gate for our connection. The customs officials decided to unpack all of the things we had purchased in Nepal for ourselves, and all the souvenirs we'd bought as gifts for friends and family. There were prayer wheels, mandalas, singing bowls, thankas, and a bunch of other shit carefully packed away in a hand-painted metal box that I'd purchased specifically to carry it all. I had spent over an hour packing everything up and was not pleased with how they were throwing stuff all over the place. Although it was clear they were intentionally being assholes, it wasn't until they found the tantric human skull that they started giving me suspicious looks. That skull was my most prized treasure, so I wasn't about to just let them start tossing it around. After having to get a little loud about how it was a sacred object, and how I didn't want them handling it, they eventually relented and returned it to me. Once they seemed satisfied they'd made a big enough mess, they finally let us through.

After getting everything repacked, we headed to the gate to wait out our three-hour layover. That was where we learned that the flight back to New York was actually three hours later the *next* day. I wasn't sure if the flight had been cancelled, or if the travel agent in New York had just neglected to tell me, but either way, we had twenty-seven hours ahead of us in Pakistan with no money. Although I definitely wasn't too excited about having to spend a night in Karachi with less than $40 in my pocket, the airline told us that they'd reserved a room for us—but when they dropped us off at some crappy hotel twenty minutes later, I realized that they hadn't really done us any favors. I used a couple bucks to buy some food from a vending machine, and then we were condemned to the room until the next day.

When we arrived back at the airport the next afternoon, one of the agents demanded some kind of ridiculous duty tax. I tried to explain that the only reason we left the airport was because our flight was delayed, but it didn't matter. Even though I knew it was just some baksheesh bullshit, I had no choice but to pay them the last bit of cash I had.

When we got to the gate, the customs official took our passports and after seeing that Karina's was Korean, he asked for her visa. It was the first time we'd traveled abroad together, and I knew nothing about her immigration status.

"Please sir, can I have Ms. Lee's visa please?" (Men don't talk to women in Pakistan.) "Visa? What visa?" I didn't know anything about any fucking visa.

"Sir, she cannot enter the United States without a visa."

There was no way I was going to leave her alone in Pakistan with no money, so I tried to explain that we'd traveled together, and since she lived in New York with me, she didn't need a visa.

This time, a bit more curtly, he said, "I'm truly sorry, sir, but without a visa she cannot get on the plane!"

Immediately after he said it, I realized that he wasn't fucking around and could tell he was dead serious about not letting her leave the country. I also knew myself, and knew that things could turn out very badly, very quickly if I let my temper get the best of me. I was after all in Pakistan. With no baksheesh. No cash. No credit card.

I took a moment to clear out all of the anger building up inside me, and tried to channel the power and energy that I'd absorbed in Nepal. I didn't want to spend one minute longer there than I had to, and knew I had to be very careful about what I said next. I held up the stub of Karina's ticket, and looked directly into the agent's eyes. Calmly, but firmly, I said, "THIS is her visa. She came here from the States with me, and she is going back with me. We are getting on this plane together." He started mumbling something, but before I gave him the chance to speak, I repeated myself even more slowly. "This IS her visa. WE are getting on this plane together."

He blinked a few times and, with a blank stare on his face, finally said, "Okay sir, won't you two please go right ahead," and he waived us through.

We started walking, and for a second I wondered if we would be stopped by security, or if it was some kind of trap, but nothing happened. We walked down the aisle and stepped onto the plane. I sat down, took a minute to get my bearings, and waited to see if someone was going to pull us off the plane. But no one did. After a few intense minutes, they shut the door, and the plane headed onto the runway.

I had done it. The Jedi mind trick. Somehow,

with the power and assistance of the Force, the Buddha, or Shiva, I'd manipulated someone else's mind into accepting my will. Maybe that sadhu at Pashupatinath had installed some magical powers into my hard drive with that tika, or maybe something had rubbed off from the Tibetan monks at Bhodanath. Maybe it was just a combination of everything I'd learned from K.C. I didn't know, but despite the dreadful prospect of suffocating on another smoke-filled twenty-something-hour flight, we were both relieved to be heading home.

***

When we arrived back in New York, the woman wound up getting detained because of an expired green card, and I had to call my dad to drive over to JFK and lend me a few hundred bucks to get her released. (Thanks, Dad.) But it didn't matter. Despite the crap we had to deal with on the trip back, I felt different. I felt powerful, grateful, and enriched—like I had left with something more than just some dead guy's intricately decorated skull. I was ready to take on the world...now I just had to figure out who the professor was.

THE PACIFIC NORTHWEST

I met Purdy sometime in the early nineties through a mutual friend. The word was that he had some mushrooms for sale, and at the time I was always in the market for a little psilocybin. He was from Oregon, and was living in New York while going to some kind of recording-engineer school. Although I had, on the rare occasion, been confused for one, I normally didn't like hippies. And Purdy was a hippie. A real crunchy, vegan-eating, dreadlocked white-boy hippie. Despite this, we had one thing in common that was enough to build a friendship on at the time. We were both cannabis connoisseurs.

Back then I was in the weed business, so almost everyone I associated with smoked weed. There were probably thousands of people in the boroughs who sold weed, but I was part of a small contingency of about a dozen dealers who had cornered the highest end of the market. The herbal elitists. While you'd think that a city of 7.5 million would have had a larger network of high-end dealers, in the early 1990s there wasn't. And the people who were all knew one another. We traded the highest-quality strains available at the time: the HP-13 (hash plant), the Sour Diesel, and, of course, my specialty, the Chronic. I know that name has since become a general term for high-end weed, but in 1992 it was a specific strain. And it was killer. This was the stuff that wholesaled at almost five hundred dollars an ounce. There just wasn't a lot of it around, and back then it was worth more than gold.

When I first met Purdy, he was still known as Josh. I eventually renamed him Purdy after we discovered a mutual admiration for the great drummer Bernard Purdie. But that was later. That first day, I was just supposed to be picking up some mushrooms from him, but to be polite I asked if he wanted to smoke. He replied with something along the lines of, "Maybe. Whatcha got?" Now when someone is a real pothead, and I'm not talking about the occasional smoker, but someone who smokes all day, every day, is prepared to decline an offer to smoke, they are a weed snob. And I could appreciate that.

So after I opened my bag and showed him what I was carrying, he started getting giddy—like how a depraved leprechaun might get around a pot of gold. He was *oohing* and *aahing* and wasn't shy about showing his enthusiasm. After I gave him a bong hit, he sighed a long breath of relief, like someone who'd just had their first drink of water after being stuck out in the desert. Then he started bitching about how hard it was to find really good weed in

New York. He showed me the crap he had been getting, and said he'd even had to resort to occasionally buying stuff with seeds!

After eyeing me up and down to make sure I was on the level, he ran over to a corner of the room and pulled out a little box from under his bed. He then proceeded to remove a little jar, and opened it to show me what he was accustomed to smoking. Inside were a few small buds about the size of peas, and despite being pretty dried out, I could tell it was good shit. He treasured them like precious stones, and told me the name of each little gem—the crown jewel something called Dogshit—and how they were all he had left of his old supply from Oregon. He said he saved these little bits for special occasions, and it was obvious few people ever got to see his secret stash. Since he probably had less than a gram of his beloved herb combined, he must have hedged his bets on something good coming from the fact that I was carrying a big bag of the super-kind shit.

While I didn't have any doubt that he was especially friendly because of my potential to be his oasis in a desert of mediocre herbs, he was a charming guy and I liked him. The next time we got together, my woman met his woman, and they got on with each other as well. His girl was some spaced-out dancer named Dreamweaver, who kept a bunch of rats as pets. Despite being pretty out there, she was a likable chick, and we all started hanging out a lot together.

I was living out in Brooklyn at the time, and

Purdy had a little place on East 7th Street in Manhattan, not far from McSorley's Ale House. Any time I was making my rounds in the East Village, I would stop by and bring him a little of whatever killer shit I had on me. Even if I didn't have anything extra primo for sale, and even when he didn't have any money, I would always hook him up with a little something—even if it came from my own personal stash. Every time I brought him a little treat, he would become super animated and start talking in different voices, and would make strange little head movements, like some kind of schizophrenic elf. I thought he was a funny guy.

One day after he finished up with school, he mentioned that pretty soon he would be moving back to Portland. I wasn't surprised. I knew that the pace and energy of New York was never really his bag. He found the city too aggressive, and I knew he missed his family and friends. We all agreed to stay in touch, and Purdy and Dreamweaver told us we should come out to visit after they got settled. He assured me that if we did ever come out, he would repay my keeping him hooked up with the kind, in kind.

***

A few months after he left, he called to tell me his buddy had just harvested a crop of the Dogshit, the famed dark brown chocolate sativa hybrid that he was always carrying on about, and invited me and the woman to visit them in Oregon. I thought it would be fun, so I booked a flight a few weeks out. I had never been to the Pacific Northwest, and was looking forward to the trip. Plus, we had a few things for them that we had picked up in Nepal.

A few days before we were scheduled to fly out, I got a call from Purdy telling me there was a bit of a "drought" going on. He, of all people, knew how important it was to make sure I'd have a nice supply of kind bud, especially when I was going to be on vacation. In those days, I could barely function without weed, and he knew it. He tried to tell me that his buddy, the grower, was dry, and that he didn't know what he was going to do. After he dropped a few hints, we established that the problem was essentially money. Ultimately, it came down to the fact that since he was broke, he couldn't assure me that there would be plenty of bud when I arrived.

After years of saying how Oregon always had a ton of great weed, he was basically telling me that the one time I decide to come out and visit, there wasn't going to be anything around. This, after making sure he never went one day without the KBs the whole time I knew him in New York. The last thing I wanted to worry about was having to travel with my own supply. It wasn't that I didn't have plenty of good shit; I just hated the idea of having to carry it on the plane. Plus, half the reason I booked the flight in the first place was because he'd just told me he had helped harvest the Dogshit!

I should have canceled the trip, but since I had already bought the plane tickets and made all the arrangements to get away for a while, I chose to suck it up. It wasn't just about the money; it was the principle. Reluctantly, I told him I would send him a couple-hundred bucks, so long as he could assure me that something killer would be waiting for me. He promised there would be. I was a little pissed about being put in that position, but decided to let it go since the week I was going to be there was also his birthday.

***

The night before the flight, I spoke to Purdy, and he assured me that we were going to have an awesome time. He said he had made plans to take us down to Eugene, and had even arranged some time for us to mess around at the recording studio he was working at. While that was all fine and good, I only cared if everything was "cool." He said it was, and told me to bring a guitar.

The next day, the woman and I packed up our carry-ons, and I decided to grab my Hofner bass. Six hours later, we landed in Portland and were met at the gate by Purdy and Dreamweaver. Everyone was all smiles and hugs, and we headed over to their apartment. They showed us around the place, and Dreamweaver held out one of her disgusting rats for Karina. After we went through the whole pleasantries routine, I finally asked the big question:

"So! Let's see what you got for us?"

Josh, who now wasn't Purdy anymore, started giggling nervously. "Eh, ah, well…"

MOTHERFUCKING elf HIPPIES! Now, I may have been a long-haired guitar player, but I sure as hell wasn't some fucking pushover pussy. I could be very generous. I would have happily shared everything he was supposed to have bought. I would have even let him "hold onto the fucking bag," as if he was the man, but, motherfucker, show me some fuckin' weed or give me back my goddamned money!

After listening to some bullshit about what had happened—i.e., he had smoked it all—it took everything I had not to kick his fucking hippie ass all over the place. What was I supposed to do? I was three-thousand miles from home, and my flight back wasn't for another week. He told me that he had saved a little joint that could get us through the night, and said not to worry, that he would figure something out. I didn't say another word, but I was fuming, and everybody knew it. I hadn't even been in Oregon for an hour, and I was already regretting the whole trip. Who the fuck keeps rats anyway?

***

The next day, we drove over to Jamison Square, essentially Portland's version of Washington Square Park, and I watched as Josh ran around trying to score some herb. After a half hour, he came back with about two grams of some shitty street weed that he claimed he had paid fifty dollars for. I knew he had no more money, and told him that this was some real bullshit.

He started asking me what *he* was supposed to do, like somehow I was the one being an asshole, forgetting that he would call me every ten goddamned minutes any time he ran out of weed back when he was living in New York. Finally, he mentioned that we could drive down to Eugene, where he "might" know someone who could hook us up. That was when I lost it.

"What do you mean you *might* know someone? New York may have been too 'aggro' for you, but there was ALWAYS something around!" I asked him what would happen if we got to Eugene and he couldn't find anything, and he had the nerve to tell me we could just go camping or something…was he fucking kidding me? "I just flew three thousand miles, and you're trying to tell me I might not get any weed? Fuck no!" I said. "I don't care if it's your fucking birthday. I don't care who you wanted to visit, what you wanted to do, or where you wanted to go—we are going to find some good weed!" I just refused to accept that the issue was over.

After trying to come up with some different ideas, I remembered some things I had read in *High Times* about British Columbia. Supposedly, Vancouver was turning into an up-and-coming Canadian version of Amsterdam. Josh said that he'd never been there, but had heard the same thing. There were supposed to be some "coffee shops," and they were reputed to be pretty much legal. Despite the fact that Josh had no money, and I knew I would have to pay for the entire trip, I didn't give a shit. At least there was hope…something to strive for. Maybe this trip could be salvaged after all. I told Josh to call whomever he was supposed to visit in Eugene and say that the plan had changed. I didn't care if I was being a dick. We were going to Canada.

We threw our bags and my bass into the trunk of Josh's little piece-of-shit hatchback and hit the road. We had three hundred miles ahead of us, but so long as we were getting out of godforsaken Portland, it didn't matter. By the time we got into Vancouver, I was getting in a better mood. I thought soon we'd be walking up to the counter of the Bulldog and looking over a menu of some of the finest herbs west of the Netherlands. All we had to do was find it.

After getting some conflicting directions, we finally made it and quickly realized there was no menu and this definitely wasn't Amsterdam. There were a few guys smoking from an old-school soldering iron vaporizer, but they were a little guarded about where the weed came from—and they definitely weren't sharing any of it. It was obvious that there was weed somewhere, but apparently you had to "know" someone to get it.

I gave Josh some money, and we split up. We each went on a hunt, and agreed to meet up in an hour. I hadn't had to score weed off the street for ages, and wasn't having much luck. Everyone was suspicious, treating me like I was a cop or something. Maybe they could sense my negative vibes, or maybe I was projecting some bad aura or energy or *something*, but one thing was for sure—I was running out of patience. Fuck you, *High Times*.

When me and Josh met back up, he'd apparently had better luck than me. He was so crunchy to the core that he couldn't have passed for a cop even if he had tried. Maybe they could smell the patchouli that emanated from his bones, or could see the bugs that lived in his dreads, but whatever the reason, I didn't care. I was just thankful he hooked up. He got about a quarter ounce, which was plenty, but it was just some mediocre commercially grown hydro. I didn't travel across the country for some half-assed buds. At that point, it wasn't just about having enough weed—it was about finding the bomb. The Holy Grail. It had become an obsession. It was now my destiny!

After we found a hotel, I sent Josh out again to try and find the green-crystal-covered sticky skunky brass ring that seemed to be tantalizing my brain, but just out of reach. He came back a little while later with something that was slightly better, but just not IT. They were both decent-grade herbs that most people would be more than happy with, but they just weren't special…they weren't grown with love. I can make different analogies comparing weed to fine wines or cars, but unless you have developed the particular taste for it, it's probably hard to understand. Although we had way more than we could possibly smoke, I just couldn't quit yet. I was not going to be defeated.

I remembered that a friend of mine in the network back home had once mentioned knowing someone in the area who supposedly grew something *really* good. I called Teddy and told him my situation. He knew a guy in Victoria, and said he would give him a call for me. Five minutes later, Teddy called me back with his telephone number. I called the dude up, got his address and the directions, and told everyone our new objective. No one was stupid enough to challenge my plan.

***

The next morning, we checked out of the hotel and headed toward the ferry for Victoria. On the ride across the Swartz Bay, I was lucky enough to see a whale not far from the boat. It was a sign—we were going to find the SHIT. I really felt hopeful about completing my mission. And since Teddy was a real aficionado, his recommendation held a lot of weight.

When we got into Victoria, we drove through an area that was seemingly right in the middle of nowhere. The directions were perfect though, and eventually we found the house. After being invited inside, the grower brought out a huge two-gallon Ziploc bag filled with dank pale green nuggets covered in white crystals. The strain was something he called White Rhino, and it was fantastic. I bought about a half ounce and we rolled up a couple of huge joints. I was finally high. My quest was over.

The next two days were spent sightseeing around Victoria, smoking the White Rhino. It was a pretty place, but I was tired, and ready to go home. Everyone was sick of one another, and I was done being reliant on Josh for transportation. I think I might've even had my flight back to New York changed to a day or two earlier than originally scheduled.

The day that we were getting ready to go back to Portland, I made sure that nobody was carrying any weed with them. Despite having quite a bit left over, there was no way to finish it all. I knew the prospect of having to throw out weed was daunting to Josh, but since we were supposed to take the ferry back to the States and would need to clear customs, I just wasn't prepared to take any chances. I told everyone to go through everything: their pockets for a loose stem or seed; the ashtray for a roach—everything. I didn't need to end this vacation with a trip to jail. When we were confident that we were clean, we smoked one last joint and headed off to the Port Angeles ferry.

When we came into port, all of the cars funneled into two lines to cross the border. The customs officials were casually waving all of the cars through as we were slowly making our way toward the gate. Every car was just driving into Washington with no problem, but when it was our turn to pass, they took one look at us and waved us out of the line and into a sectioned-off area.

I knew it. Josh, with his stupid-looking knitted Rasta hat; and Weaver, with her perpetual "I need a miracle" look; and me with my Asian girlfriend. I fucking knew it. I wasn't at all surprised that we were targeted, but I knew that since we had cleaned everything out and taken every precaution, we would be fine.

They told us to step out of the car, and asked us some generic "Do you have any illegal drugs, weapons, or explosives in the car?" questions, to which, of course, we replied, "No." The next thing we knew, they were unscrewing the hubcaps and bumpers, taking apart the panels, and looking under the car with all sorts of mirrors and flashlights. After going through our luggage, one of the agents asked who the guitar belonged to. I told him it was mine. He said that they didn't like to handle musical equipment and asked if I could open the case while he inspected the bass. I said it was fine and, as I walked over to the agent, told him, "I know how we look. We're not idiots…we wouldn't be so stupid to try and carry anything across the border." He said nothing as I opened the case…he just stared. I repeated myself: "I know how we look. You don't need to worry…" and basically acknowledged that yeah, we knew we fit the profile. We were the types to do drugs, and because we knew we would probably get pulled over, we wouldn't be trying to bring anything with us.

After the agent carefully looked over the

bass—inside the f holes and everything—he asked me to open up the pick case, which is basically a little case within the case where you can store guitar picks or strings. When I opened it up I saw, or thought I saw, a little Ziploc bag filled with about an eighth of the genuine NYC Chronic. Not sure if this was actually happening, or if my eyes were playing tricks on me, I repeated myself one last time: "I know how we look...we wouldn't be stupid enough to try and bring anything across the border..."

Time stood still and I felt like Obi-Wan Kenobi. *These are not the drugs you are looking for.* We were both just standing there, staring right at it. I looked up and could see that his eyes were blank. After he blinked once or twice, I started to close up the case, and he asked me to step back behind a line that was painted on the pavement.

A few minutes later, the agents started packing everything back up, threw our bags back into the trunk, and began screwing the bolts back on the car. When they finished putting everything back together, they thanked us for our cooperation and told us we could go. We all got back in the car and, without looking back, started driving through the gate.

I didn't say anything to anyone. I had to think and try to figure out what had happened. Was this another test? Only a few months earlier, I had managed to get Karina on the plane in Pakistan without a visa, but even then no one was ever at risk of actually being arrested.

After a few minutes, I decided what had happened. I had done it again! Even though I probably wasn't ready to lift a spaceship out of a Degobah System swamp, I had perfected the Jedi mind trick! This was proof that I must have absorbed something in Nepal. I had the customs official so convinced he was wasting his time that the weed became invisible to him. I'd somehow managed to create a blind spot in his mind's eye. Of course, it was also possible that he did see it, and decided it wasn't worth doing all the paperwork for an eighth of an ounce, but I don't think so—I like my first theory better.

I probably couldn't have pulled it off so well had I actually known it was in there. But then I started to wonder if maybe it really *wasn't* in there...that maybe I'd Jedi mind tricked myself! Maybe I had just imagined that I'd seen it. How could I have carried it all the way from New York without knowing it? Could it be possible that I'd had it the whole time—that I'd carried it over air, land, and sea? Across multiple states, and even into another country in search of the perfect bud...without even knowing it was there?

After about ten minutes of pondering the question, and confident that we were far enough away from the border, I finally told Josh to stop the car. Everyone asked me what was up, but I just told them I had to check something in the back. Before I said anything, I had to make sure that I wasn't going crazy. Josh pulled the car over to the side of the road, and I hopped around to the trunk and opened the case to my bass. And there it was. The falling sun shone one last illuminating beam directly onto it, and it was glowing like the Holy Grail. It was the Chronic.

It was old, and had probably been sitting in there from some rehearsal I'd had ages ago. Normally you could smell it from twenty feet away, and it was so sticky that if you threw it against a wall, it would stick...but this old weed, despite being very dried out and brittle, was still the Chronic. I got back into the car and held up the bag. Everyone's eyes widened, and Josh turned back into Purdy the elf and started giggling and jerking his head around all weird. I told everyone what had happened, and no one could believe it. We didn't have anything to smoke it with because we'd thrown out all the rolling papers, but I crumbled up a bud and poured it into a cigarette that I had emptied the tobacco from. We lit it up, smoked it, and despite its age, still got higher from it than anything else we had smoked the whole trip.

After an uneventful ride back to Portland, we finally got back into town late in the evening. We had a flight booked back to New York for the next day, and I told Josh to just drop us off at a hotel near the airport. After some halfhearted protests that we should save our money and go back to their apartment, to everyone's relief we just decided to head to a hotel and bid our farewells then and there.

Despite the fact that I never got to try the infamous Dogshit that Josh had been bragging about for years, he still had the nerve to ask me for a little bud of the Chronic before we separated. Fucking hippies. I think the last thing he said was something about paying me back in a few weeks, but of course that never happened, and we never spoke again.

CENTRAL AMERICA

Not long after returning from Oregon, I received a collect call from Ossining Correctional Facility in upstate New York. Jerry was in the middle of serving his sentence in Sing Sing for the mushroom bust, and since I was one of the few people who would accept his collect calls, he got in the habit of calling me a few times a week. Normally he just wanted someone to talk with in order to relieve the boredom, but this day was different. He told me about a book being passed around by the inmates that supposedly explained the details of a secret war being waged by the US government against the American people. Not only did it explain why people were systematically being incarcerated for nonviolent drug offenses, but it also explained that everyone's personal freedoms were at risk. If the plan described in this book was ever fully realized, it could mean the end of the world as we knew it. Since the book was banned inside the prison, he told me it was up to me to find a copy on the outside. I needed to figure out what was going on.

After I got off the phone with him, I wondered if the end-of-times scenario described in this book could somehow be connected with the visions I'd been having since I was eight. Not a day had passed that I hadn't thought about my mission to save the world; the problem was I never knew exactly what I was saving it from. If this book could shed light on a specific threat, it could help me figure out what I was actually supposed to do. Up until that point, it had only been a feeling…a premonition. If this book existed, it could be the key to my destiny!

I immediately began searching the shelves of all the major bookstores in New York. Not only did none of them have it in stock, they basically told me that since it wasn't even listed in their databases, it didn't exist. *How convenient.* Next, I began a search of all the independent bookstores, of which New York had more than probably any other city in America, but still I had no luck. No one had ever even heard of it. If it wasn't for the fact that Jerry had said he'd seen the book, I wouldn't have believed it actually existed.

Right when I was about to give up, I passed by a table on St. Mark's Place that was covered with used books, most of them looking like old paperbacks that someone had found in the trash. Just as I was starting to walk away, I heard someone call out, "Hey professor!" to the old black man standing behind the table. I looked up and noticed that he was staring directly at me. *Professor??*

"Hey boy," he said. "You lookin' for a book?"

I told him I was.

"It's about time," he said. "I been waiting for you for a long time!" He bent over, reached under the table, and began rummaging through some boxes. When he stood up, he held out a slightly worn paperback and asked if this was what I was looking for. It was THE BOOK!

I started asking questions, but he just shook his head and told me we were running out of time. I hurried back to my apartment, locked the door, and dove straight into it. Just a few pages in and I could barely believe what I was reading.

The book was the manifesto of a man who had uncovered the mother of all conspiracies. While serving as an officer in the US military, he had inadvertently discovered that the American government was actually being run by an ancient secret society. They, in turn, were carrying out the will of an advanced race of aliens on a mission to take over the world. By installing a network of cabal banking establishments, they were able to control all of the world's economies and ultimately global politics. By manipulating humanity into believing that we were approaching a new era of world peace, also known as the New World Order, they had established a complex system of mind control that prevented people from realizing that we were actually on the brink of an apocalypse. A polar shift was soon approaching that would melt the ice caps, and in turn kill off a majority of the world's unilluminated population, thereby leaving the Earth open to repopulate with their own alien species. It all made perfect sense...

Now that I had all the information, I just had to figure out a way to stop it. Determining if everything would happen at once, or over a series of events was impossible to tell. The clues were supposedly spread out all over the ancient world, with especially pertinent information seemingly locked within the pyramids. If I could break the codes, I might be able to find the answer—but I was running out of time. From what I could gather, it seemed that the ruination of man would start with Y2K, when all the computer systems would shut down. Following that would be a planetary alignment on May 5, 2000 that would kick off the natural disasters. The final end date seemed to correspond with the end of the Mayan calendar, so I decided that would be the best place to start.

I found a flight that was scheduled to leave in less than a week. I headed up to a travel agency in Midtown and, after picking up my ticket, stopped at a few stores to grab the proper apparel. Most of the clothing I owned was not suited for tropical climates, so I found a few pairs of lightweight cotton pants and some thin linen shirts. Since I hadn't spent more than five minutes in the sun in years, I made sure that they were long-sleeved. To complete the getup, I stopped at a hat store and picked up something that was a cross between a fedora and a cowboy hat. It looked like something that would have been worn in the Australian bush at the turn of the century. I was tempted to go full Indiana Jones and buy a brown Stetson, but decided that might be a bit *too* over the top. Despite my initial temptation, it was also for this reason that I didn't buy the pith hat. After all, there was no time for foolishness. I was on serious business—a mission to save the world—not to look like some character on a tiger-hunting expedition.

***

A few days later, I boarded a plane at JFK, and after a quick layover in Miami landed in Belize City. Calling it a city at all was a bit of a stretch. It was, for the most part, a total shithole. I had read somewhere that British Honduras, the colonial name for Belize, was once described as the armpit of the world. Five seconds after stepping off the plane, I was able to see why. I had a cab take me to a hotel that was not only considered the best, but was at the time the only actual hotel in the entire city. I think it was a Raddison. After checking in, I pounded a few drinks at the bar and tried to come up with a game plan.

The next morning, while eating breakfast, I saw a sign advertising cheap PADI certification courses. While I knew that I really shouldn't let anything deter me from my mission, I decided getting a scuba-diving license for fifty bucks was too good a deal to pass up. Besides, I figured one day it could come in handy—you never knew when you might need to strap on some tanks in order to explore a lost underwater city...or at least that was what I told myself.

My dad had been a diver, and when I was a kid I loved to hear about his tales from under the sea. He had an old picnic basket filled with stuff he'd collected when he was exploring shipwrecks back in the seventies. It was mainly a bunch of coral and broken shards of pottery, but to me it was sunken treasure. I probably could have gotten certified at any time in New York, but who wants to pay a fortune to learn to dive in cold, murky water? Belize was not only cheap, but the water was warm, crystal clear, and teeming with life. After paying my bill at the Radisson, I walked down to the pier located right in front of the hotel and caught a boat to Caye Caulker, an island renowned for its tropical beaches and reefs.

When I boarded the water taxi, the sun was not yet fully up. About halfway through the journey, sunlight started dissipating the thick fog and illuminated the sea into a gleaming turquoise. When the island came into view, it looked exactly like the posters you might see hanging on the walls of a travel agency. For the first time, I thought maybe I understood the appeal of this kind of place—palm trees swaying in the breeze, people casting lines and nets from small boats, and little bungalows with grass roofs lined up along the shore. Maybe this really *was* paradise.

***

There were no cars on the island, but after we

unloaded on the dock, there were a few golf carts waiting for passengers. I didn't yet know where I was staying, but a dreadlocked golf-cart driver said he could take me to the perfect spot. After driving less than fifty yards to a little bamboo hut, he called out loudly to a woman who started pulling me out of the cart before I could protest. I was taken to a small hut, with a tiny bathroom off to the side, which was considered high-end for the island. The walls were mainly open, and there was no electricity for most of the day, but it was super clean, had a hand-carved lacquered bed and table, tropical hardwood floors, and a solar-heated water tank for the shower. It was perfect.

I dropped off my bags and walked over to a little bamboo bar with a grass roof that was set up on the beach. I ordered some big tropical drink and tried to relax, but I couldn't. Back then I could never understand why people would want go on vacation just to sit by some water and do nothing for a week. Although I get it now, halfway through my first drink I was already getting restless. Since it was still early in the day, I figured I'd walk around the island a bit. After finding the little dive shop that offered certification classes, I signed up for one that was scheduled for the next morning. Even though I'd missed that day's class, there was a boat getting ready to go out to the reefs for a snorkeling trip. When they said they still had room, I paid for a spot and jumped on.

It must have been obvious to everyone that I was new to the island. I was white as a ghost, and was still carrying around a kind of high-strung energy that was foreign to the place. A woman asked me if I needed any sunscreen, and despite the fact that couples were applying thick coats of the white paste onto each other's bodies, I politely declined the offer. Even though I'd always hated the greasy feeling of sunblock, when someone else offered me their bottle a few minutes later, I took it as a hint and reluctantly accepted the bottle...then squeezed a quarter-sized amount in my hand...and carefully dabbed it on my face like I was delicately applying makeup.

We untied the boat from the dock and headed out to a place called Shark Ray Alley, where nurse sharks and rays were swimming around in relatively shallow water. After hopping in, we were literally swimming up to the creatures and touching them. I should have noticed that even the sharks were red, but I didn't. After a while, we went out a bit farther and anchored by the reef. Aside from nature shows, it was my first time seeing brightly colored fish and corals outside a fish tank. I was so taken with the beauty of it all that I completely lost track of time. The boat didn't seem to be in any kind of a rush either, so I stayed out in the water snorkeling for hours.

Eventually one of the deck hands called out that it was time to head back, and everyone started climbing back onto the boat. Someone mentioned that I was looking pretty red, but I was too stupid to give it much thought. There probably wasn't much I could have done at that point anyway. After swimming for hours, the damage had already been done—I had essentially been cooking myself alive.

The truth of how serious it was didn't begin to register until we reached the shore about an hour later. When I got off the boat, I felt a little tightness behind my knees, but walked back to my bungalow still mainly unconcerned. It wasn't until after taking a shower that I began to notice that something was really wrong. I walked over to the mirror and, for the first time, saw what I had done. Looking head-on at my reflection everything appeared totally normal, but after turning around I could see that I was fucked. The front side of my body was completely white, but the back half was as red as a stop sign. It looked so ridiculous and unnatural that I had to laugh at myself for a minute. It was the last time I would laugh for days.

I tried to lie down, but it was too painful. I couldn't sit in a chair because I couldn't fully bend my legs or lean back. It was also difficult to stand up straight because it felt as if my skin had tightened around my body like shrink wrap. For someone who usually didn't leave the house until dark, I don't know what I was thinking. I guess I'd assumed that since most of my body was underwater, I would be protected, but it wasn't until later that I learned that the water actually magnifies the sun. Exposing myself to the rays for almost five hours in the dead middle of the day, so close to the equator, without sunscreen, was apparently just asking for a disaster.

Even though the hut had a gorgeous view, it

was impossible to enjoy the scenery. No matter what I did, I just couldn't get comfortable, and it was getting worse by the minute. I hadn't really had anything to eat or drink all day, and I was starting to feel dehydrated. Since there was no phone or room service I knew I'd eventually need to head out, but waited until the sun was all the way down before I decided to make my move.

My entire back, and the backs of my arms and legs, were so badly burned that even with only a bathing suit on, I could barely move any part of my body. With slightly bent legs, and a hunched back, I crept down a little dirt road to the nearest restaurant. People literally cringed when they saw me coming. Some shook their heads in disbelief while others just turned away in disgust. I tried to order some food from an older Creole woman who, with a Caribbean accent, said, "What done happen'd to you, boy? You look like you been cooked up like a crab!" A younger girl just smiled at me like I was the dumbest white boy she had ever seen. I tried to eat some fried fish with a beer, but after the walk didn't have much of an appetite. Everyone was having a good time, drinking and laughing, but I was in too much pain.

I hobbled back to the bungalow and tried to find a bearable position, but it was impossible. I couldn't lie down on my back, and everything hurt too much to even stretch out on my stomach. All of a sudden, I started to feel sick and began throwing up the little bit of food that I'd managed to eat. One minute I'd get the chills, and the next would be burning up. Suffice it to say, I didn't get any sleep that night.

I couldn't spend another minute like that, so the next day I checked out of my idyllic beachside bungalow and crept back down the road in search of a room with an air conditioner. But the only one I could find was a dingy, windowless hole with exposed cinderblock walls. Although it was the complete opposite of the quaint little hut I'd just left, I was past the point of caring about aesthetics. It had cool air, and I figured it was the best move I could make. It also had a bath.

I bought some aloe vera, water, cigarettes, and a few boxes of oatmeal from a small convenience store, and retreated to my new hovel like the Hunchback of Caye Caulker. I was a hideous, disgusting creature, so offensive to lay eyes upon that I figured the only thing I could do for the benefit of humanity was hide. I tried to contort my body into a position where I could apply a little of the aloe onto my own back, but it was impossible. I even wrapped an aloe-soaked T-shirt around the end of a disgusting toilet plunger, and stood on the tips of my toes trying in vain to get some relief. Since my Achilles heels were so beyond burnt, that too failed miserably, and I just wound up convulsing in pain like an epileptic. No matter what I tried, it was useless. Eventually I just gave up and started sobbing uncontrollably.

It was all my fault. I'd tried to enjoy one leisurely moment in the ocean, and Kinich Ahau, the Mayan sun god, had taken his revenge. What business did I have trying to have fun when the world needed saving…I had no choice but to pay for my transgressions.

I was all alone in a foreign country with no one to even help me put aloe vera on my back, so I filled up the filthy tub with cold water, poured in the oatmeal, and crawled in the bath. With the exception of when I needed to lean over the toilet to either vomit or piss out my ass, I sat in that tub twenty-four hours a day—even sleeping in that fucking thing—and pitied myself for the next five days without seeing or speaking a word to anyone.

I don't know if it was sunstroke, or sun poisoning, or what—but I was SO sick and in SO much pain that I would just sit there and alternate between praying to, and cursing, God. There I was, in a place most people would consider paradise, trapped in a disgusting little room with nothing to distract me from the pain, except the enormous bugs that I watched crawl across the fucking walls. "*I'm sorry!*" I cried out. "I repent… I REPENT!"

By the fifth day, my fever started to break, and I tried to venture out to eat something. Even though I still couldn't walk fully erect, I finally was able to regain some mobility. There weren't a lot of people on the island, but the few kids who lived there laughed and pointed at me like I was a leper and called me Slim Shady. A teenager tried to sell me some ganja, and even though I knew it was some kind of uncured bush weed that wasn't even remotely related to the cannabis plant, I bought it anyway. Sure enough, it was unsmokable.

Although I had made a little progress by managing to actually leave my dungeon for fifteen minutes, I knew that after another day of sitting in that bathtub I would surely lose my mind. I had to get off of that island. The next morning, I slowly tiptoed to the only travel agent on Caye Caulker. When I stepped through the door half naked, the woman working inside let out a gasp and said, "Oh my God—what happened to you?" I stood there for a minute, unsure of how to reply. She was a kind middle-aged lady, with kind eyes, and a kind face…and seeing that I was obviously a mess, walked up to me and put her hand gently on my arm and asked me how she could help. It was the first time anyone had shown me any compassion in over a week, and I suddenly wished that she was my mother.

I told her I needed to get off the island immediately. Then I almost started sobbing while telling her that I was all alone, that I had nobody to help me put lotion on my back, that I'd been confined to a bathtub for days, and that the local children had laughed at me and called me Slim Shady. After patiently listening to my insanity, she said I could hire a puddle jumper to get off the island. It would take me to the airport in Belize City, and from there I could get a flight back to New York.

After thinking it over for a second, I decided I wasn't going to let my own stupidity put an end to the trip. I was on a mission! I had to pull myself together. I hadn't come all the way to Belize to spend my entire trip crying in a dirty bathtub. "No!" I said. "I must go to the jungle!" That was, after all, the reason I was there. I should have known better than to stop off at a tropical island...I wasn't built for that kind of environment.

She looked at me like I was crazy. "Well, where do you want to go then?" she asked, and I told her I needed to go to the pyramids. To Tikal, the ancient Mayan city in Guatemala! She made some phone calls and after a few minutes told me the arrangements were in place. There was a little airstrip, she said, and a plane would be waiting for me at noon the next day. I thanked her and headed back to my room, eagerly awaiting my chance to escape.

***

The next day, I hobbled over to the airstrip, where I was met by the pilot. There was another couple already sitting in the backseat of the plane, and the pilot said that before we went to Guatemala we would be dropping them off in Belmopan. I asked him where I was supposed to sit, and he told me that I would be sitting up front with him.

The skin on my back had taken on a blueish-purple color with a texture that most closely resembled bubble wrap. I had huge blisters filled with pus covering nearly half my body, and that morning had actually been the first time I'd put on clothes since I'd arrived. I carefully climbed into the cockpit, and tried to keep from crying out in pain. The pilot told me that I had to sit back and put on the seatbelt—but since my face looked normal, the nature of my problem wasn't apparent to anyone else. There was no way for him to know that I hadn't leaned against anything for almost a week...that I'd been living suspended in an oatmeal soup bath like a low-budget Jedi.

Everyone was waiting for me to sit back and buckle up, and I knew he wouldn't take off until I did. I had to suck it up—I had no choice. I knew I'd die if I had to spend another day on that island, so I held my breath and leaned back. I felt all of the blisters pop in succession, until the back of my shirt, and the seat, were soaking wet with pus. I had to bite my lip to keep from screaming.

He started up the Cessna and took off down the runway. I was never so glad to leave a place as I was that island. I looked down at the sandbar covered in palm trees, and cursed its existence under my breath. Every time we hit turbulence, I would freeze up and cringe. When the pilot noticed the look of sheer terror on my face, he told me that I didn't need to worry—he hadn't crashed a plane yet. After I explained that I was not afraid of flying, I could hear him laughing over the sound of the engine, and although I wasn't sure, I suspected he would occasionally jerk the plane for good measure. After about a half hour, we landed in Belmopan to drop off the couple sitting in the back. Then it was just me and the pilot the rest of the way to Tikal.

As we were flying low over the canopy of the jungle, I tried to imagine all the exotic life forms underneath. A diverse assortment of plants and trees, birds, snakes, jaguars, and monkeys doing their thing the same way they had been for thousands of years. For a moment, I felt hopeful that maybe the world was still healthy and thriving, but eventually we passed over enormous areas that had been cut clear, or slashed and burned to the ground—like gigantic scars upon the face of the Earth—and I remembered why I was there.

***

After about two hours, we landed in Flores, the airport closest to the ruins. I got my visa, converted my money into pesos, and caught a cab into the heart of Tikal National Park. The entrance had a few lodges, and a cantina where the paved road ended. After checking in at one of them, a porter showed me to my room. While standing outside the door, I felt something hit me in the head, and when I looked up there was a monkey that had dropped some kind of fruit rind on me. Instantly, I was cured of my past week in hell.

I was so excited to be there that I dropped off my bag and immediately headed out to the ruins. I felt virtually no more pain. Shortly after starting down the trail, I heard the most terrible screams coming from howler monkeys, high up in the trees. The whole forest was alive with sound. There were monkeys and birds screeching and hollering all over the place, and ring-tailed coatimundi walking around, strange animals that looked like a cross between a lemur and a raccoon. I hadn't even been on the trail for ten minutes when I saw a toucan fly by me. A fucking toucan! I couldn't believe it. The only thing that could have made the whole scene any more unbelievable was if Tarzan himself had come swinging by on a vine.

After a short hike, I reached a small clearing and got my first glimpse of the central acropolis. I was awestruck. Tikal! The lost Mayan city! When I got closer to the main plaza, my mind was flooded with visions of how the place would have looked fifteen hundred years earlier, when it was a pre-Columbian metropolis, a center for culture, art, science, and human sacrifice. It was magical.

Strangely, there was hardly anyone around. There were places you could stand, amid the ruins, covered in vines and surrounded by the lush jungle, without seeing another human being. The pyramids were over 150-feet high, with steep stairwells—perfect for rolling severed heads down during sacrificial ceremonies. There were hieroglyphic-infused stelae, with images of gods and beasts carved directly into the rock. Even though I couldn't decipher the characters, I somehow had to make sense of it all. I knew there was still life and power in those stones, and could sense that there were clues everywhere—I just had to figure out a way to find them. The fact that I had absolutely zero archeological training was not going to stop me.

Was it possible that the dark magic of the Mayan death cults was still alive? That it had somehow managed to survive the demise of their city and culture, still lingering within these ancient monuments of their achievement? And if so, would we all ultimately be subjected to the same fate? Destined to repeat the same end? Was our debt too great to forgive...no other way to repair the damage of our transgressions? To restore the natural balance of the world, did our mother need to swallow us back up and reclaim our civilizations with the plants and animals and jungles and forests that came before us?

Or was it not too late? Could I somehow prove myself a worthy ambassador of humanity? To be deemed worthy by Ah-Puch, the Mayan God of Death, in the hope that he might choose to communicate with me and give me some answers—a key to our salvation!

***

The next day, I went out exploring a bit farther, well past the main plaza. Tikal was more than just a few pyramids and a ball court...it was a whole Mayan city, where hundreds of thousands of people once lived. The remnants of their civilization were everywhere; it's just that most of it has been reclaimed by the jungle. I climbed up a little hill and found what looked like a small manmade cave. It was pitch black inside, and I heard a strange noise that sounded like a growl. I couldn't see anything, but was smart enough to know I should probably walk away.

I kept walking farther away from the acropolis and as the ruins became more and more obscure and spaced out, the jungle kept getting thicker. As an ex-Boy Scout, I was pretty well versed in the virtues of being prepared, but that day, I became so engrossed in the place that I was just wandering around aimlessly, walking wherever something caught my eye. I had been out there for hours, and when it started to get dark, I had to admit to myself that I was lost as shit. I took an inventory of my situation and figured that since I was walking around in flip-flops with no supplies, things could get pretty interesting if I had to spend the night out there. I knew that so long as I could avoid a run-in with a jaguar, I would probably be okay, but the mosquitoes were coming out in force. Not only that, but I was also out of water, so I decided my best bet was to just pick a direction and keep walking.

About an hour later, the sun was almost completely down. It had been hours since I'd seen anyone, and I couldn't remember the last time I had been on any kind of path. I kept walking until I passed through some more trees and suddenly found myself practically face-to-face with four or five men who didn't look like they were expecting visitors. They were carrying lamps and digging in the ground, and then I noticed that two were also carrying rifles on their shoulders. If they were on official excavation business, they certainly didn't look like archeologists. I assumed they were out there illegally hunting artifacts because they didn't seem too pleased to see me.

They began speaking to one another in Spanish, and I had no idea what they were saying. Probably something about how easy it would be to cut me up and bury me in the hole they were digging. I tried to show how distressed I was with body language, and in my extremely limited Spanish, said, "Salida? Donde es salida?" They just stood there and stared at me. I didn't know if they wanted to kill me, or just thought I was a stupid gringo, but eventually one of them pointed in a direction that I hoped would be my way out of the jungle. I said "gracias" real friendly-like and started walking.

After about an hour, I came out onto a clearing that appeared to be a trail, and a few minutes later I was back in the Grand Plaza. There was no one around, and I had all of Tikal to myself. The moon was high and almost full, and the light was reflecting off the Jaguar Temple in a way that illuminated it perfectly. Aside from a few howler monkeys making some noise off in the distance and the cicadas and crickets playing their nighttime symphonics, it was pretty quiet. I tried to imagine sitting all alone in Times Square a thousand years after the apocalypse...what it would look like...how it would feel. I hoped something would speak to me—a Mayan god, a jaguar, an alien...anything. I waited. I needed a sign. Something to let me know I was not wasting my time, something to let me know there was still hope. But nothing happened. Eventually my thirst got the best of me, and I walked out of the park and back to the lodge.

***

The next morning, I checked out with a desk clerk who looked exactly like the Mayans depicted in the stelae. He had a cone-shaped head and was a bit cross-eyed, both features considered a sign of beauty to the ancients. Although I doubted it had been done intentionally—the way it would have been by Mayan parents at one time—I assumed he would have been considered a real looker around these parts back in the day. While I wasn't sure if he was still the pussy magnet he might once have been, he was nice enough to direct me to a bus stop that could get me back to Belize.

***

The bus was old and run down, but completely empty when I got on it. I thought, *Okay, this won't be so bad*, but within a half hour there were literally so many Guatemalan people on the bus that they were sitting on top of the roof, on top of one

another…and eventually on top of me. Somehow, at every stop we made, even more got on. I quickly regretted trying to save a few bucks by not taking a cab, but the border we were heading to in Belize had a few ruins that I wanted to check out. It was hotter than hell, though, and the smell was becoming tremendous. I managed to stand up, and squeezed as close to a window as I could get.

At one point, a Caribbean guy with dreadlocks came on the bus with a gigantic *Wild Style* eighties boom box. I was the only gringo, and he was the only black guy, and we exchanged a quick look acknowledging each other as being the two odd men out. After a few minutes, he pressed play on his tape deck and this funky beat and bass line started up that I'd never heard before. It kinda sounded like a funky reggae interpretation of "Sherry" by the Four Seasons—and while I have no idea who did it, and haven't heard it since, it grooved like a motherfucker. It was so good, it made the whole ride worthwhile. Not long after it ended, my friend got off the bus, and it seemed like he'd showed up from dub heaven to play that song just for me.

Afterward, the bus came to a stop on a stretch of unpaved road somewhere between two jungle-covered mountains. I looked out and saw that we were surrounded by a bunch of mean-looking dudes dressed in fatigues and carrying machine guns. After a minute, two of them jumped on the bus and started shouting at the passengers. Everyone started to panic, and I thought we were about to be robbed, until they started going through everyone's papers instead. I knew the country had some political issues, but I had no way of knowing if these guys were looking for rebels or if they *were* the rebels. All I kept thinking was, *Great, someone is going to have to tell my mom I was taken hostage in the middle of the Guatemalan jungle.* But after a little while, they must have been satisfied that we were not who they were looking for and waved us through.

When we finally made it to the border near San Ignacio, I hired a taxi to take me to Cahal Pech and the pyramid at Xunatunich. Although El Castillo had some elaborate hieroglyphs, ultimately neither could compare with the majesty of Tikal.

Before I left Belize, there was one last place I wanted to check out, and that was the ruins at Lamanai. It was difficult to get there, but eventually I made it to an archeological research station that had a few rooms available to rent out to visitors. I think it is now more geared to tourists, but back then I was the only "guest" that was not doing some kind of "official" research. It was a pretty isolated site and had some interesting ruins, the most well-known being a huge stone carving of a face called the Mask Temple. *Lamanai* means sunken crocodile in Mayan, and after going out on a boat with flashlights the night I arrived, I was able to see how it got its name. Golden eyes floating just above the surface of the water, lots of teeth beneath.

There was a little mess hall with a bar, and after

having a few drinks with some biologist, we wound up on the topic of drugs. We discussed all the compounds that have been or have yet to be discovered in the jungle, and all that could be lost if we continued to cut it down. Eventually the conversation turned to psychedelics, and we talked a bit about ayahuasca. While Belize didn't have the necessary plants, trees, and vines to make yage, he did mention that frogs with psychoactive properties were everywhere. I had heard of this...

The toads were called incilius campbelli and they were part of the Bufonidae family. After asking him to identify them for me, I decided I would try to catch one. We were both pretty drunk, so while I was rolling around on the ground trying to catch the little fucker, the biologist was looking at me like I was insane. Finally, I got my hands on one and stood up so we could look it over. When I asked him what I was supposed to do next, he admitted he was no expert, but did confirm that in addition to secreting the psychoactive ingredient, the frogs are also poisonous. Like a fucking idiot, I held it up to my face and started licking its back.

I figured since he was a scientist, he could verify if I was doing it correctly, but, laughing hysterically, he admitted he had no clue. Since I didn't have the slightest idea either, I decided to give it a few more licks for good measure even though it was terrible. I could definitely taste some kind of chemically alkaloid component, and figured that was a good defense against being eaten, but I wasn't sure if it was going to work. I was aware that I was intentionally trying to ingest poison, but in my semi-wasted state I wasn't overly concerned. I had come all the way to the jungle and still was just as clueless as to what I needed to do to save the world. I figured this would be my last chance for answers.

I went back up to the bar and took a few shots to clear the taste of frog out of my mouth, until everything seemed to be spinning. Before long I felt like I was gonna be sick, but wasn't sure if that was just the effect of too much tequila. I eventually stumbled my way back to my bug-infested room and crashed on my foam bed.

***

The next morning, in addition to a hell of a headache, I woke up with a strange pain in my foot. At first I assumed I had been bitten by something, but it was slightly swollen and kind of numb and tingly—and different from the countless mosquito bites all over my body. With a slight limp, I made my way to the cantina for some food, and found the biologist I'd hung out with the previous night. He asked how my toad experience was, and though I told him I couldn't remember much, I asked if he had ever heard of swollen feet being a side effect. He looked at my foot and agreed that it definitely didn't look good; but there was no hospital for miles, and even if there was, I probably wouldn't have gone anyway.

My flight back to New York was scheduled for the next day, so I decided it was time to head back to Belize City. My foot was getting more swollen, and I couldn't have done much exploring even if I had wanted to. I could tell that the person who ran the lodge was starting to get seriously concerned when he offered to drive me to the nearest doctor, but I politely declined, thanked him for his hospitality, and asked him to call me a taxi instead.

When I arrived back in Belize City, I had the driver take me to a bed-and-breakfast recommended by the people at Lamanai to try and get some rest. By the time I was ready to head back to the airport the next morning, my foot had swollen to the size of a football. It was also starting to turn a red-blue-purplish color that was beginning to get me a little worried, and even after adjusting my sandal strap I still wasn't able to get my foot inside. It was getting even harder to play it cool when I had to hobble through the airport with one of my feet bare, but despite people offering me assistance, I just wanted to get home. Between the sheets of skin still peeling off my back, the thousand mosquito bites, and the swollen foot, I must have looked lovely.

***

Back home later that night in NYC, it was hard to imagine where I'd been just a day earlier. Judging from my dog's power sniffs, she couldn't either. Just as I was deciding if I should head to the ER, the swelling started to decrease. Although I still had no answers, I was relieved that I might actually be able to live out my days with two feet—and even more relieved that Ah-Puch, the Mayan god of death, had decided to spare my gringo ass once again.

LOS ANGELES

After traveling around searching for answers and coming up with nothing, I decided I had to try a different approach. If the end was soon approaching, I figured I could waste no more time exploring exotic foreign locations. I had to get down into the mud, to the epicenter of evil—a true living cultural wasteland. It was time to go deep into the heart of darkness...Hollywood, California.

I flew to LA pretty frequently, usually to work on music with some players I knew out there, but this time was different. This time, I couldn't remain detached. I had to breathe it all in and let the evil seep into my veins. I knew the effects that California could have; I'd seen the degeneracy and corruption infect many good people. The disease ran rampant out there, and I knew I couldn't go raw dog so long as I was still wearing the psychic prophylactics necessary for survival in New York. I could no longer remain immune. I had to willingly let myself get infected if I was ever going to discover its dark secrets. There seemed to be two paths to help speed up the immersion. Kale, or cocaine. Since my body naturally rejects vegetables, I chose the coke.

One of my friends hooked me up with a dealer named Carlos. Whether you are in New York, California, or Colombia, there is always a dealer named Carlos. I bought an ounce of shitty cut coke and got to work. I went to all the shows at the dives on the strip, hung out with all of the hipsters in the bungalows of Laurel Canyon, and went to pool parties at the Chateau Marmont. I even went to the juice bar at the Erewhon natural market. I was getting close to the source...I could feel it.

More bullshit was being thrown about than a gang of coprophiliac cowboys: *"I hooked up a deal with him and them to do this, and my script is getting picked up by so and so to do that, and they think my idea for a reality show based on how fantastic my whatever is..."* just went on and on. All the signs that I was in the right place were there. The fall of Rome was coming.

***

On New Year's Eve, 1999, I went to a Y2K party at some fabulous movie star's house in the hills. It was supposed to be the night the computer systems crashed, and everyone was excited. The idea was everyone would get fucked up out of their minds and celebrate. When the electrical grid shut down, we would watch out over the valley as the lights went off and the world went dark. There was ketamine, LSD, mescaline, Mexican black tar heroin, booze, and of course, cocaine. Someone laid out a huge pile of blow on a CD in front of a fan, and I watched as it blew all over the room. A huge cloud of coke went into the air and slowly settled into the carpet. The starlet's dog came and sniffed a bunch of it off the rug and began licking the white powder off its snout. It quickly started running around in circles and began pissing all over the house. Things were off to a good start.

It was almost midnight, and as the clock counted down a strange combination of cynicism and excitement emanated throughout the house. I tried to watch people's faces to try and get some kind of insight into what they were thinking…what they were feeling. Although, the only thing anyone seemed to be afraid of was that nothing would happen… That we would find ourselves in exactly the same world at 12:01 that we were in at 11:59—and this was the real tragedy. There would be no more waiting for some external event to force us to examine our lives, what we had been doing, and what we had become.

Sure enough, when midnight struck, nothing happened. No one was relieved. They were disappointed. I was disappointed. The whole time that I had been thinking I needed to save the world, I really had no idea what I would be saving it from. None of the grand conspiracies really mattered. All we had was ourselves. We still had to wake up at some point every day and face in the mirror whatever it was that we'd become. And then suddenly I realized that everything was just as it should be…exactly as it was *supposed* to be. A fucking mess that we'd created.

There would be no easy way out.

No salvation.

May 5, 2000 came with the same anticlimactic fanfare. Nothing happened. But although I couldn't put my finger on it, something still didn't *feel* right.

JERUSALEM

I was on a layover in Switzerland, waiting for my transfer, when the interrogation began.

"Why do you want to go to Israel?"

"Are you Jewish?"

"Do you know there is a war going on?"

Being hassled by customs was nothing new, but I had never been interrogated by an agent before even stepping foot inside their country. It seemed like they wanted to dissuade me from visiting.

"Do you know anyone in Israel? Why should you want to go to Israel if you are not Jewish?"

After the third round of questioning, I figured I would go along with them. "Fine," I said. "If you want to get technical, isn't Judaism passed through the mother's bloodline?"

The agent tilted his head, as if observing me from another angle would somehow give him some better insight into my intentions.

I decided to play the game. "Well, my great-great-grandmother on my mother's side was Jewish."

With a skeptical, but interested look, he asked, "What was her name?"

When I told him, he said it didn't sound Jewish. I said it was because she was married. Her maiden name, however, was Rosenshwartzweissburgman-and-goldstein!

He definitely knew I was fucking with him at that point, but thought it was funny. Luckily, most Jews have a sense of humor. At some point I did tell him the truth: that like many New Yorkers, I did have a few Jews in my family, but wasn't Jewish myself. I told him the main reason that I was visiting was to bring my father to Jerusalem. I opened my backpack and slapped a Ziploc bag full of ashes on the table in front of him. He couldn't argue with that. He still insisted that it wasn't a good idea, and that it was a bad time to visit, but I knew he was going to let me in. At the very least, I had convinced him that I wasn't a terrorist. My family was Catholic, for fuck's sake. At the time, I thought the process and scrutiny was ridiculous.

My father had passed away a few months earlier, after a nearly yearlong struggle with cancer. We had talked about going to Jerusalem before he died, but never actually made the trip. He had convinced himself that he was too sick to travel, and despite my argument that the worst thing that could happen was he'd die, in the end he didn't go for it. Regardless, I thought the trip might still be a good way to get some closure. Neither of us was even remotely religious, but for reasons that are still hard to explain, I had to take him there.

Not long after being diagnosed, the cancer started to manifest itself in some pretty nasty ways. He couldn't eat, and he was in a lot of pain. Fortunately, when doctors know you are going to die, they generally don't get stingy with the painkillers. First it was the oxycodone, then the MS sulfate pills, and eventually a liquid morphine solution called Roxanol. Even though he was taking a lot, there was so much around that I started ingesting my fair share as well. While the morphine definitely helped ease some of the emotional craziness, I knew that I would have to clean myself up after he died. For better or worse, I had to face the fact that life went on. The apocalypse hadn't happened, and I was only twenty-five years old. I had to get on with it. I came up with a plan to stop off in the Middle East for a few days, and then meet my band in Thailand to work on some new material. Jerusalem was supposed to be nothing more than a quick detour.

The welcoming committee at Ben Gurion greeted me with a screwdriver and a pair of pliers. In the never-ending name of security, I watched as they carelessly dissected my Gibson SG. Eventually they handed it back: the body in one hand, the neck in the other—held together by loosened strings flopping around like the dismembered ligaments of a mutilated cadaver, the pickups hanging out by only their wires. After shrugging off the look of horror on my face, they were kind enough to wave me through the security gate.

I caught a shuttle into Jerusalem and made it to St. George's Cathedral right after nightfall. I had planned on renting a room there, so I jumped out and rang a bell since the gate was already closed. As I was strolling around waiting for someone to open it up, I noticed that the driver was starting to look a little apprehensive. It turned out that we were in a Palestinian neighborhood, and the driver didn't feel safe waiting in an alley in the dark. I hadn't been in the city for five minutes before the intense day-to-day realities of living in the Holy Land became apparent. When someone finally came to open the door, the driver sped off like a bat out of hell.

***

The next morning, I picked up some sesame bread from a street vendor and headed down into the Old City. It looked like an ancient fortress, the whole area enclosed in immense walls that looked ready for battle. When I first walked through the Damascus Gate, it felt like I was entering a time warp. As I walked through the twisted narrow alleyways, past the little shops, I got a sense of how the world must have felt hundreds, if not thousands, of years ago.

The Old City is broken up into quarters: Jewish, Muslim, Armenian, and Christian, and I tried to explore them all. Eventually, I made my way over to the Dome of the Rock and the

Western Wall by the Temple Mount. Since the dome seemed to be closed off to non-Muslims, I sat by the Wall and closely watched everything that was happening. People were literally rocking out, praying, and singing songs in Hebrew. As I walked closer to stick my own note into the Wall, I could see that these people were bound together by some kind of ancient brotherhood, pilgrims from all corners of the earth united in their belief that they were God's chosen people. The energy was manic and frantic, joyous yet cautious—and so delicate, like it could all fall apart at any minute. And then I watched as the guards threw kids up against the walls, frisking them, always on the lookout...making sure that no one would dare try to disrupt the fragility of the moment. They had made it for three thousand years, and they sure as hell weren't about to let anyone stop them now.

Stepping into the Old City is like doing a stint in prison. Your identity gets stripped down to its most basic components. Nobody cares what you think or what you believe, so long as you identify with one of the established factions. You either stick with your own tribe, or you're on your own. Based on proximity and family history, I became a Christian. As much as I wanted to believe that we can all get along in an ideal world, I quickly realized that when three of the biggest religions are all fighting for the same turf, you either choose a side or prepare to get caught in the crossfire.

I was amazed that all of these places, places that are considered so holy to so many, could somehow be crammed so close together. Separated by piles of rock. I struggled to understand how these people could all theoretically be praying to the same god, yet hate one another so much. They may have different prophets professing different interpretations, but at the end of the day it was all the same bullshit. But the one thing I couldn't deny was that *something* was there. You could feel it. An energy that was undisputedly powerful, but not necessarily benign. It wasn't like the energy I felt in Nepal; none of the mutual respect of the Hindus and Buddhists. Everything in Jerusalem just felt tense. I couldn't help but wonder if it was the holy places themselves, or the people who worshipped at them that had created the energy in the first place.

And this was the paradox I found myself dealing with. As much as I had been enchanted with the mysticism of the East—the simple and obvious truths; the philosophies that made total and complete sense in my mind—none of it could ever answer the pain in my heart. It was easy to comprehend that life is suffering, but it was not so easy to accept. I wondered if there was some genetic flaw in my European DNA that refused to come to terms with this kind of acceptance…something in me that wanted to fight! To fight and shape the world around me, instead of just accepting my circumstances. Even though there was a kind of madness, a reckless insanity that propelled me forward, it was the madness itself that gave me a small glimpse of hope…this idea that if

I just kept pushing things a little bit further, eventually I would find my salvation. This was the Passion of Jesus, and I didn't need to rationalize it one bit. I understood it in my body, in my blood, and in my soul.

When my father got sick, I began to understand that there's a hole that can only be filled with religion. My father didn't have that comfort of faith when he was dying, and I almost wished he had, even if for no other reason than to diminish some of the pain that is inherent in death. And even if all of the pieces didn't add up in my mind, the power of Jesus was calling out to me. Like Fox Mulder with the UFOs...I wanted to believe.

I decided to stop at an antiques dealer, and felt compelled to buy a fifteen-hundred-year-old Byzantine cross. Aside from a brief phase at thirteen years old, when I wore rosary beads and a black velvet jacket in a pathetic attempt to emulate some convoluted idea of a Goth, I hadn't worn a cross since my First Communion. Regardless, I bought the cross, and some military-grade bootlace from an Israeli army surplus store, and double-wrapped the cord with the cross around my neck.

***

I woke up at the crack of dawn the next morning and walked over to the Garden of Gethsemane, by the Mount of Olives, and looked down at the walled city to the west. I thought that somehow, from a distance, I might be able to put everything into perspective. I decided to retrace the steps of Jesus, and followed the Stations of the Cross on the Via Dolorosa, through the way of suffering, and walked down through the Lions' Gate to enter the walled city for the last time. Although the cross I was carrying was not large, wooden, or heavy, I still felt a tremendous weight on my back. I didn't know what it was, but I was sure something was wrong.

As I walked along the Stations of the Cross, I tried to imagine the scenes leading up to the crucifixion of Jesus. By the time I made it to the Church of the Holy Sepulchre, I was exhausted.

When I was in Rome as a kid, I remembered being blown away by the grandeur of the Sistine Chapel. I couldn't help but notice that every inch of the place was carefully designed to invoke a feeling of awe. The Church of the Holy Sepulcher had none of that. From the outside, you could walk right by without a second thought, and would never know it is the most important place in Christianity. Despite the fact that Christianity has more followers than any other religion in the world, that day there was almost no one around. I assumed there weren't many tourists around due to the high-security alerts, but inside I found it virtually empty. None of the bustle like at the Dome or the Wall. Aside from a couple of priests going about their business, I had the whole place to myself.

After looking at it from the outside, it turned out to be much bigger than I had imagined. There were artifacts and chambers spread out over a chaotic floor plan, and you could tell that it had been destroyed and rebuilt multiple times. Originally it was a temple dedicated to Aphrodite, some say initially built to conceal the tomb of Jesus. Constantine turned it into a church in 335 A.D. because he believed it to be the location of the last four Stations of the Cross, including the places where Jesus was crucified and buried. Since then it has been run by priests from a multitude of Christian denominations known as the Status Quo. Nothing gets done without the approval of the different factions. There is a ladder on a ledge by a window that's been there for over 150 years because no one can agree what to do with it. Despite the politics, it was beautiful inside.

After exploring all of the different chambers, I finally came to the place where Jesus's tomb was supposedly buried. I took out my father's ashes and poured them into a crack between the marble slabs that covered the tomb. Suddenly I fell to my knees and began to cry out loud. I didn't just shed a silent tear...I was sobbing uncontrollably. It was the most intense feeling I had ever experienced. I was so overcome with emotion that I became practically hysterical. I knew I had to pull myself together, but couldn't shake the feeling of unbearable loss and pain. It wasn't just the pain of losing my father—it was something bigger...like thousands of people were crying out at once.

I looked up and noticed that two nuns were walking past me. They didn't bat an eye, as if they had seen long-haired tattooed freaks crying hysterically at Jesus's tomb a thousand times. They just walked right on by, like the scene I was putting on was the most normal thing in the world...and then, just as quickly as they had appeared, they were gone. And once again, I realized that I was all alone. Not just alone at the tomb, but alone in the world.

After I was finally able to get a grip on myself, I left the church to try and figure out what the hell was going on with me. I had heard there was a phenomenon called the "messiah complex," where people who come to Jerusalem begin to believe they are the reincarnation of Jesus...and start wearing sandals and robes and shit. The problem was I didn't know if I was just feeling the spirit, or if I was losing my mind. I had come to Israel just to drop off some of my father's ashes and to try and clear my head. This was supposed to be a fresh start...Whatever insanity was looming in the streets of Jerusalem, a city that had been a hotbed for religious fanatics and madmen since antiquity, I decided I wanted no part of it. Not at that point in my life. I needed to get out of there before it was too late.

***

I caught a shuttle bus back to the airport in the early afternoon. Right before we pulled into Ben Gurion, the driver made a quick stop to pick up two women. As they got on the bus, they asked the driver if he had heard anything about what had just happened in New York. I turned around and asked them what they were talking about, and they said that just before getting on they'd heard that a plane had hit a building. Then they mentioned something about a transmitting tower or an antenna, but didn't seem to know too much about it. I thought about it for a moment, but figured it wasn't that big of a deal.

When I got to the customs desk at the airport ten minutes later, the woman who was working the counter must have seen that my passport was issued in New York. She looked up at me with concern and asked me if I knew what was going on. When I told her I didn't know what she was talking about, she said there were big problems, and directed me to a TV that was set up in the middle of the terminal. I noticed that people seemed to be running around frantically, but I just couldn't process what was happening. It felt like I was in a dream and hadn't woken up yet.

I saw a crowd gathered around the TV, and ran toward it to see what was going on. I couldn't believe what I was seeing...One of the towers at the World Trade Center looked to be on fire, and then literally within two minutes of getting in front of the screen, I watched as another plane came into the frame and smashed into the second tower. It was 4:03 p.m., September 11, 2001. At that moment, everyone's worst fears were confirmed: this was no accident. And then all hell broke loose.

Everyone remembers where they were on 9/11, but the whole thing for me was beyond surreal. It was the only time in my life that I think my body went into some kind of shock. I had been living in downtown Manhattan, just a few blocks from the Twin Towers, for years. I saw the buildings from my apartment window every day; I had just seen them standing two days earlier. I had watched as the smoke came up from the towers after the first attack in 1992, and here I was watching it again. But this time was different. Everything seemed to be moving in slow motion. It was like watching a family member get shot. After a few minutes, I began to snap out of my daze, and realized that everyone was going crazy. The Israelis wasted no time in deciding who was responsible—they didn't need to wait to hear any facts from some reporter on television. They were sure they already knew who was to blame, and they looked like they were ready to go to war. It was starting. The madness had begun.

All I knew was that two planes had just crashed into buildings a few blocks from my home, and I was supposed to be catching a flight to Cairo within an hour. I ran over to a pay phone and tried to call my girlfriend and mother in New York, but all of the lines were either busy or down. I tried to find out when the next flight was leaving for New York, but nobody could give me any definitive information. I ran around like a madman, adrenaline pumping, but my objectives and goals were not clear. I found out that my flight to Egypt was delayed, so I ran back to the television. Fifty-six minutes after the South Tower first got hit, I watched as it collapsed. And then something in me broke.

I wondered if this could really be happening, if this was the moment I had imagined for so many years...could the premonitions be coming true? Everything I had felt at the Church a few hours earlier now seemed to make total and complete sense. I didn't know if there were going to be more attacks, and if so, where I should be going. I thought that after all of my self-inflicted psychic-warrior training, I should have been prepared for this, but I wasn't. I realized that I didn't have the slightest idea what to do. I knew that thousands of innocent people had just died, and my heart was breaking. Was this really the beginning of the end?

After that, everything became a blur. I wandered back to my gate, and the security guard actually tried to dissuade me from flying to Egypt because it was an Arab country. He believed if World War III was going to break out, Egypt probably wouldn't be the best place to be. Two days earlier, they'd tried talking me out of coming; now they were trying to talk me out of leaving. Time was running out, and I had to make a decision. Someone overheard that I was from New York and shouted at me, "Now you know what we live with every day!" I tried calling my mother one last time before they started boarding the flight, and she picked up. She said she had spoken with Karina and that everyone was okay. I had to decide, if a war did break out, would I want to be in the first country to get bombed, or the one that would possibly be launching them? I remembered the Book said there were answers in the pyramids, so I figured if I couldn't get back to New York, I would take my chances in Egypt. When I approached the gate again to board the plane, the agent told me I was crazy.

It didn't matter anymore. I *was* crazy. Everything was crazy. One day earlier, I'd thought I was just about to put the insanity behind me, but apparently it had all just begun. I was in shock, and so confused I barely knew what I was doing. When I finally sat down on the plane, everyone who had seen me losing my mind outside of the gate began to stare. There was an engineer from Europe who wound up sitting next to me. He was living in Cairo while he worked on some irrigation project, and he offered to let me stay at his house until I figured out what I was going to do. It was a nice offer, but I decided I needed to be alone.

EGYPT

When I landed in Cairo, I had a cab take me directly to a hotel called the King James. I checked in as quickly as possible and ran up to my room to put on the news. Al Jazeera was showing a nighttime bombing raid on Afghanistan that I don't believe was ever shown in America, and the BBC kept showing the planes crashing into the towers. Each time I watched it, over and over again, it felt like I was getting stabbed repeatedly in the chest.

The next morning, I called a bunch of travel agencies to see if I could find a flight back to New York. Not only could I not find one, but I learned that all flights into the States had been grounded indefinitely. It was still early in the day, and I realized that if I sat in the room watching the planes crash into the towers one more time, I might have a nervous breakdown. There was nothing else I could do to get home, so I did what anyone else would do while in Egypt. I jumped in a cab and went to the pyramids.

The Sahara Desert seemed to creep right up to

the edge of the city. From a distance, it is hard to differentiate where one ends and the other begins—even the bricks used for the buildings are made from the same sand. When I first saw the pyramids, I could tell that they were immense beyond anything I could have imagined, and thought it would be interesting to see a terrorist try and take down one of those fuckers. Even after almost five thousand years, it probably wouldn't have left much more than a dent. I walked around for a bit, trying to take everything in until I found a "guide" who offered to show me around on the back of a camel. I took him up on his offer, and we walked around the site. I wasn't sure what I was looking for, or what answers I might be able to decipher in the pyramids, but figured since I was already there it was worth a try.

Far from the tourists, my guide took me to a secret chamber that I'm sure was supposed to be off limits. The entrance was covered by a drift of sand and was so narrow, I had to crawl on all fours to get inside. There were still some hieroglyphics legible, but unfortunately pretending to be Indiana Jones didn't help me decipher them any better than the ones in Tikal. We passed an old cemetery, and of course the Sphinx, but I still had no better insight into what was happening. After checking out everything I could possibly see around the pyramids, I bought a ticket to enter Giza…also known as Khufu, Cheops, or the big one. There was a long corridor that was so tight, I had to crouch down just to walk through it. It led to a burial chamber that had been emptied long ago, where I poured out a bit of my dad's ashes. I could feel there was still power in the stones, but like Jerusalem, I couldn't tell if it was benign. All I could feel was suffering. The Book discussed a number of different theories as to how the pyramids were built—ranging from a hydraulic elevator system to being assembled by alien technology—but however they did it, I felt pretty confident that a bunch of poor fuckers died in the process.

After about a half hour, I went back outside and noticed that the Byzantine cross was missing from my neck. I knew the cord couldn't just break, and it definitely couldn't have fallen off—there was simply no explanation for what could have happened. It was as if the pyramid had magically swallowed it up. I thought there must have been some meaning, but couldn't figure it out. I wasn't sure if I even cared anymore. I tried to just accept it as being another mystery that was beyond my reach, and after a while decided to head over to Saqqara and a few other nearby sites.

***

Later that night while having a beer at the hotel bar, I met two local Egyptian guys named Nasir and Mohammed who were living at the hotel. They were students at the local university, and just based on the fact that they were drinking, I knew they were pretty progressive by Egyptian standards. I felt comfortable enough to speak freely with them, and after talking for a while about the attacks on the WTC, they invited me to go smoke something called Bango with them. I'd never heard of it before, but didn't waste any time lighting up after I watched Nasir roll up some kind of dried-out plant matter into a joint. It was harsh as hell, and was definitely different from cannabis, but I didn't give a shit what it was so long as it helped me not think. Afterward, they suggested we get some tea at a hookah café where they supposedly had some good apple shisha. After about eight or nine drinks, and the Bango, I was almost starting to feel okay.

The café was in a neighborhood that I could tell didn't get a lot of foreign traffic. The clientele consisted exclusively of men who were drinking tea and smoking, and after finishing the hookah, I stepped into an alley to get some fresh air. Two men with long beards and *kufiyas* wrapped around their heads followed me outside. One of them had his hand on a knife that he was carrying around his waist, and although I normally don't take shit from anyone, I knew I was about to have a problem. I could tell by the way they were smiling that they meant trouble. Right as I was trying to decide if I should run or attack, my two new friends came out and intervened. They started yelling at one another in Arabic, and although I had no idea what they were saying, I could tell it was serious. Nasir and Mohammed came up and grabbed me by the arm and told me we had to go. They told me these men didn't like Americans. I asked who they were, and they whispered that they were Qaeda al-Jihad. At the time, I didn't know what that meant. I had never heard the term before, but assumed they were some kind of Egyptian mafioso. It was the first time I had ever felt absolute hatred just for being an American, and suddenly I realized that *I was* the infidel.

***

The next morning, I was walking through the Khan el Khalili bazaar, one of the oldest *souks* in Cairo, when a voice came over a loudspeaker and called out to everyone from the nearby mosque. I watched as all the men laid out their mats, kneeled down, and began their salah. After their prayers, everyone resumed their business, but since there were very few tourists around, the vendors all began aggressively hawking their wares to me. Most were extremely friendly, but I could tell that something wasn't right. I managed to get through the stalls with a polite "la shukran" at every advance, but I knew I had to get out of there. I was standing out in a bad way. I decided to stop telling people I was American, and for anyone who asked questions, I replied in broken English with a heavy Italian accent. I found a travel agency to see if anything had changed about getting a flight home, but there was still nothing. I contemplated trying to change my flight to Bangkok for an earlier date, but decided I would wait it out a bit longer. I bought a plane ticket to Luxor instead, in one final attempt to find answers.

The Luxor and Karnak temples are situated close to each other on the upper Nile River, like some gigantic open-air museum. The ruins are filled with amazing columns and statues that seem designed to dwarf the human stature. Some of the columns are over sixty-five feet high. There are gigantic obelisks and rows of sphinxes. While nothing can compare with the pyramids for sheer size, the overall diversity of the architecture in the ancient city of Thebes is in many ways much more impressive. It gave a better idea of just how sophisticated their ancient culture must have been. There are hieroglyphics carved into everything, but, even after exploring every little corner of this ancient world, I was still no closer to discovering any great revelation about the present. The only thing I knew for sure was that nothing lasts forever, and that even if a plane hadn't destroyed the Twin Towers, they still would never have survived as long as everything in Egypt. Regardless of all the technologies developed in the past five thousand years, nothing can beat stone for permanence. And even stone can't save a culture from itself.

I was desperate for answers, but knew there wasn't a human being on the planet who could help me. I wanted to pray to someone, to something...anyone. I had no real faith in Jesus. I had no faith in Allah, or even in the God of Abraham. I had no faith in Horus or Ra. I had to accept that I plain and simply had no faith. I didn't know if I had lost it, or if I'd never even had it. The only one I had ever believed in was my father, and now he was gone too. I took a boat out into the Nile and poured the rest of his ashes into the river that had given life to this once-great civilization, and talked to him in the hope that maybe he was listening—but I didn't hear anything back.

***

After a few days in Egypt, the time finally came for my flight to Bangkok. There still were no flights into New York, and despite my concerns about getting even farther from home, it was time to get out of the Middle East. I knew that the majority of the people there were honest, decent, and hardworking, but it had come out that some of the terrorists who attacked the WTC were Egyptian, and the tension was growing greater every day.

It had only been about a week since I had left New York, but I knew nothing would ever be the same again. I was homesick, but couldn't go home. It wasn't just knowing that the buildings that had always towered over my shoulders were gone. It was that my home was wounded and hurting, and I couldn't be there to mourn with my people. I've never felt such a strong connection with a specific tribe, or felt pride about being from a certain place…always thinking tribal mentality was mainly primitive and divisive. I had never really considered myself to be anything specific. Maybe it is just the luxury of white privilege, but I never thought of myself in terms of race, color, or creed. Never as a white man, or a Christian. Not as part Italian or Irish. Hell, I barely even identified as a regular red-white-and-blue flag-waving American. But for the first time in my life, I did feel pride in where I was from. I was a New Yorker…and it felt like a part of me had died.

THAILAND

When I landed in Bangkok, I was a fucking mess. Although getting out of the Middle East wasn't the worst idea I'd ever had, it felt like I had lost my sense of direction. I *was* lost. I had just been in Thailand a few weeks earlier, and while it seemed like a good place to regroup after losing my dad, now I wasn't so sure what the hell I was doing back there again. Originally, the plan was to meet up with my band and spend a few weeks writing and rehearsing some new material, but after the planes went down, all my actual plans seemed to go up in the air. I had done all of the sightseeing on the previous trip with my sister and some friends. Now it was just another big foreign city, and I was alone.

I found out a few flights had just started to open up back into the States, but my people in New York insisted they were fine and there was no reason to rush back. While it may have been true that they were physically all right, when I look back, I realize I should have been there just to grieve with everyone. At least in the Middle East I was still waiting to see what would happen next, what I would do…but to just come to the realization that this was it somehow made things even harder. Every time I turned on the TV, the only thing showing on every channel was a replay of the Towers falling. Over and over again. All of the craziness that had transpired over the last few days had been accompanied by adrenaline. Once that started to wear off, the only thing left was severe depression.

I walked around Bangkok trying to make sense of everything. Was it possible the Book had been right about the world coming to an end, but just wrong about the details and the dates? I wasn't sure about anything anymore. Was this truly the fall of Babylon, or all part of some master plan…and how did the Illuminati fit into all of this anyway? The Book said nothing specifically about New York getting attacked by terrorists. I started to question everything. For a moment, I even started to wonder if it was just in my head, if I had somehow imagined all of this. I had read about something called MK-Ultra and Operation Artichoke in that crazy book too. It described how the American government had given hallucinogens to unwitting people in some kind of psyops experiment. Was it possible that I too was actually a victim of some kind of strange psychic warfare? At the very least, it might explain where the PCP could have come from when I was eight.

But I knew it had to be real. I could feel it in my bones that something was wrong. I didn't have a playbook to deal with any of this. If this was the start of the apocalypse, it didn't feel anything like I had imagined. It just felt lonely. I didn't know what to do. All I knew was that I had somehow failed.

***

For a few days, I didn't leave my room at the Mandarin, not even to eat. Eventually I called my friend Benji in New York and asked him where I could score some dope. Benji was an international addict, and one of the worst junkies I knew. He had grown up in France, and was a descendent of the family that had created the first chain of department stores in New York. He had inherited a small fortune, but had somehow managed to blow it all on dope. At some point, he'd realized it would be cheaper to maintain his habit in Thailand, where he wound up living about half the year. He supported himself by buying Khmer bronzes and Thai antiquities that he took back to New York to sell at huge markups; then he'd return to Thailand to repeat the process all over again.

He told me if I wanted to find some dope, I would need to look for a guy named Dang who hung out around Patpong Road. Although I knew the chances of finding him based on Benji's description from ten thousand miles away was slim, it didn't really matter. Despite some vague instructions, it was just a few blocks from the hotel, and I was pretty determined. Somehow I would find someone…anyone, who could help me deal with my pain.

After passing a number of stalls covered in fried insects of every conceivable variety, I turned onto Patpong Road. The street was glowing with the same neon signs, bars, and live-sex shows I'd seen just a few weeks earlier, but this time everything seemed so dull as to appear lifeless. Even the famous "ping pong pussy show" now just seemed like some kind of artificial approximation of life. All of the excitement and intrigue was gone. The tourists walking around looked like zombies, with no real purpose other than to be distracted...distracting themselves from the fact that we were all already dead, yet still going through the motions like a recently decapitated insect in a world that was also in the process of dying... Pretending to still be alive, but desperate and lonely just like me.

There were girls hanging out in front of the clubs, trying to pick up some work. A few tried to stop me, but I wasn't interested. I was looking for something else. One girl tried to make a joke, alluding to the fact that if she wasn't pretty enough for me, then surely I must not be interested in *any* girl. But most seemed to instinctively understand because it was no secret that they were not really interested either. Not in me; not in anything. They knew we were all just going through the motions. Some looked like they had known for a long time; others were just starting to realize. But ultimately it didn't matter...the world was coming to an end.

I walked through the darkest alleys I could find. I could see the signs, as obvious as neon that junk was there. I could feel it. The problem was, just knowing it was there didn't mean that it would be available to me. I was a *farang*, a foreigner, and wasn't yet connected with the right people. I was so desperate and unconcerned with any consequences that I asked practically everyone I saw if they knew where I could score. After about an hour of this, I finally found someone who had the unmistakable look of an addict. The features of a junkie are often subtle to anyone who hasn't been an addict themselves, but were clear to me. I told him I was looking for Dang, and he told me to follow him. We walked up some stairs to the platform of a train, and he told me that *he* was Dang. I was pretty sure he wasn't, at least not the one I was looking for, but it didn't matter—anyone could have been Dang; the name was as common as John. All that mattered was that he knew where the dope was.

He told me that if I gave him 4,000 baht, he could get China White #4 for me. But this wasn't Kathmandu, and he wasn't K.C. This was heroin. A whole different game. Plus, as far as I knew, China White #4 was a myth. Just a generic term not unlike what the Chronic had become for weed—just a name that was supposed to be synonymous with high quality. There was no way I was handing him any money without product in hand, and I told him so. He said to wait on the platform, and after fifteen minutes he returned and told me to follow twenty steps behind him. I followed him into the bathroom of a shopping mall, and he went into an empty stall. I walked into the one next to him, and after closing the door, he leaned down and held out a vial with a blue plastic cap. I handed him the money, still convinced I was going to get beat, and in a second he was gone. After opening the vial right there in the stall, I started gagging. It was real dope. Even though I hadn't used any since my dad had died, my body was quivering with anticipation.

I practically ran back to the hotel. When I got into the room, I locked the door and poured out a huge line of the fine white powder. The part of my conscience that at one time would have made me stop and think twice was gone. I just didn't care. All I needed was for the pain to stop. I sniffed the line and laid back on the bed… Within seconds, I felt the warmth spread throughout my body, my icy limbs thawing as if melted by an internal fire. After a few minutes, it felt like I was floating in a warm pool, enveloped within a nurturing womb. The outside world ceased to exist, and the pain receded. It was relief.

***

The next day I got a call from my drummer Slim, who was in Copenhagen. He said he still wanted to come, despite the fact that GB2, our bass player, didn't sound like he was going to leave

New York. Slim assured me that once GB2 found out that we were both in Thailand, he would come. Two days later, I picked Slim up from the Bangkok airport, with the hope that this news would somehow change GB2's mind, but even after he'd arrived, GB2 was still adamant about not being able to leave New York. He said his girl was too scared to be left alone. After hearing this, I started to feel guilty, and couldn't help but wonder if I should have been there too. I didn't know what to do, but Slim insisted we just needed to give it a little more time...and so the wait began.

Despite not knowing what the fuck I was doing or which way I should be going, I found myself in the position of having to show Slim around Bangkok. While our initial plan was to head up to Benji's house in Chiang Mai, we had some time to kill until we knew if GB2 was going to show. Short on ideas, I decided to take Slim over to Wat Po to see the huge golden reclining Buddha. For a few minutes I contemplated the statue, and wondered if he was lying down in acceptance or resignation. As we were leaving the temple, we saw a street vendor selling T-shirts of Bin Laden with the World Trade Center burning in the background, like some vendor selling unauthorized merchandise outside of a Britney Spears concert. It was impossible to make sense of it all.

***

Later that night, I took Slim over to Patpong Road to see the "sights." I knew him well enough to know that this wasn't really his scene, but I was out of ideas. Eventually we found our way into a bar, and within a few minutes a couple of girls walked over and asked if we'd like to buy them some drinks. After we politely declined a few offers, a pair of *kathoey* came up to the table trying to find out what we were looking for. I had noticed they were hanging out with the one girl who never approached our table...a girl who I thought was beautiful.

One of the trannies told me the girl's name was Anne, and said that they had grown up together. I learned she was in town visiting her sister, and it was obvious she wasn't a working girl. It was either because of, or in spite of this fact, that I became even more interested in finding out about her. I asked the ladyboys if they thought Anne would let me buy her a drink, but was told probably not. Despite this, when their group was getting ready to leave, one of the ladyboys came by our table and asked if we would like to come hang out with them at their house.

Me, Slim, and the two ladyboys jumped in a taxi with Anne and another girl named May. Ten minutes later, we were in a small white room with linoleum flooring and bad lighting. The only things resembling furniture were a pair of foam mats laid out on the floor. They turned on a little transistor radio and started listening to a Thai pop singer called Benz, who had a huge hit with a song called "Do Re Mi." A few minutes after getting situated, May asked if we'd like to smoke some Ya-Ba, and although we didn't know what it was, we soon learned it was a form of cheap speed that was extremely popular in Thailand. Ya-Ba translated roughly to Crazy Medicine, and looked like little blue and red pills. They broke them up into tiny pieces and smoked them off small strips of tinfoil that they'd separated from the wrapper found inside a box of cigarettes. The smoke was sweet, and within a few minutes I was buzzing with a cheap speed high. Before long, it was all gone and like all amphetamines, once you get started you don't want to stop. I mentioned if they could get more I'd be happy to pay for it, and asked if while they were at it they could also pick me up some opium. They didn't know what that was until Anne spoke up and told them I was looking for "fin," which they seemed to find quite amusing—apparently opium was considered an old-man drug, and they didn't know anyone who would have it.

The dope I had back at the hotel was close to running out, and I knew I would need more to help balance out the speed. I decided having the girls hook me up would be less reckless than another street transaction, so asked if they could get me a little heroin instead. I handed one of them 2,000 baht, and she returned a half hour later with the Ya-Ba, the dope, and incredibly even some change. I couldn't believe it: an honest transvestite streetworker.

***

By the time the sun was coming up, the ladyboys had left and Slim and May were fucking on one of the mats. It was the first chance I'd had to really talk to Anne, and I learned that she was nineteen and had a two-year-old daughter. She spoke better English than any of the others, and told me that she'd been trying to find a job in Bangkok. Her daughter was staying with her family in the small farming village she had left, where the only work available was picking rice. She had hoped that by learning English she could find a better job than farming, but there wasn't a lot of work anywhere. It was then that I started to realize that most of the girls who wound up working on Patpong didn't start out as hardened street girls.

I told Anne I should probably head back to my hotel, but she told me she didn't want to be left alone with Slim and May, and asked me to stay. We tried to share the tiny mat and despite being pretty uncomfortable, I could feel there was a vibe between us. I gave her a small kiss before closing my eyes, and thought I heard her crying quietly before I fell asleep. Even though at the time I didn't know it, I realize now that she knew exactly how things were going to turn out.

The next day, as I was getting ready to head back to the Mandarin, Slim told me he was going to stay and hang out with May. I asked Anne what she was going to do, and she said she was going to head back to her sister's house. I asked if I would see her again, and although she said she didn't know, I told her I could drop her off wherever she liked. After jumping in a tuk tuk, I asked her if she'd like to have lunch at my hotel—somewhat reluctantly, she agreed. Under the pretense of me taking a shower, we went straight up to the room and within minutes started fucking like animals. We also wound up living together for the next few months.

After a few days, Slim confirmed what I had already expected: GB2 wasn't coming. It was depressing news. We didn't know if we could find another bass player to work with, but at that point it didn't really matter. Nothing did. All of my ambitions regarding my life and career now seemed pointless. If the apocalypse had started, and there was nothing I could do to stop it, why should I even care? I was no one. No one was anyone. There was no God, or saviors. No mystical realities hidden in the shadows. No magic fairy in the sky who was going to do anything to save us. I had to accept that everything I had seen, experienced, *believed*—was all just random craziness. I had to come to terms with the fact that life was just one giant shit show. Once I could accept this, I'd be free. I decided I would just try to enjoy what little time I had left. I would indulge in everything that life still had to offer—everything that I could get my hands on. The two best things I could think of were pussy and drugs, and Thailand seemed to have plenty of both. Regardless, Slim and I agreed that we needed to get out of Bangkok.

We decided to meet up in a town called Chiang Mai, where Benji the junky supposedly had a house that I'd agreed to sublet. Anne had never been up north, so we flew up a few days early to ride elephants and hang out with the hill tribes. You could visit the Karen and Lisu, who made their living selling raw opium and trinkets to tourists, and who, for a few baht, would allow you to take pictures with the women who stretched their necks out with brass rings. The whole scene was depressing, basically the Asian version of an Indian reservation. A few days later, we met up with Slim and Benji in Chiang Mai.

***

Right off the bat, Benji was not happy to see that I was with Anne. He said the whole situation was not going to end well. But after I bought his plane ticket, and got conned into paying his back rent, I really didn't give a fuck about his opinion. To top it off, when he came back from settling up with the landlord, he was already nodding off and carrying a fresh pack of syringes. Despite all of his bullshit, he took us over to what turned out to be a nice old traditional teak house with three bedrooms. Once I saw that it was fully furnished, and decorated with religious artifacts and amulets, I felt a little better about the whole deal.

We all rented scooters and went out to eat at one of the restaurants in the outdoor bazaar. Benji was so high he took a few bites of his food and started dozing off in his fucking pad thai. Although he looked like a goddamned degenerate, it didn't change the fact that I was looking forward to trying some of his dope. It turned out to be even better than what I had bought in Bangkok, and probably was the best shit I'd ever had. Still, I made sure to never get so fucked up as to make a complete spectacle of myself.

After a few days of living together in the house, everyone started getting on one another's nerves, and the vibes were getting bad. Slim was upset about the dope, Benji was upset about Anne, and I was upset that anyone could have the audacity to get upset about anything (considering the fact that the world was coming to an end). Even still, when somebody suggested that we should leave Anne at the house for a couple of days, rent a few motorcycles, and drive up to Burma, everyone agreed it was a good idea. We found a place that had a few 400cc Hondas for rent, and headed toward the Golden Triangle.

The road to the Mae Sai/Tachileik border was nice and open. I had an old 1972 BMW R75/5 back in New York, and even though the Honda had a smaller engine, it felt faster and lighter. There were very few cars around, and no highway patrol, so we were opening up and pushing the bikes pretty hard. When we got farther north, the terrain started changing dramatically, and we headed onto some back roads that ran through the mountains. That was a bad idea.

We saw a sign for some holiday palace built for the queen, and decided to take a look. We followed steep, narrow, and winding roads deep into the mountains, and after about an hour, realized we had no idea how to get back to the highway. We were driving down a road filled with tight s-shaped curves when I saw a truck coming at me. I had a split second to make a decision: crash head-on or veer off the road and risk driving over the cliff. I managed to find a little spot right between the truck and the cliff, clipped the side of the pickup, and went down.

I skidded out about twenty feet into a tree and when the bike and I finally stopped, we were inches from the edge. After narrowly passing the truck himself, Slim knew I was going to be in trouble when the pickup came around the bend. Amazingly, aside from some cuts and bruises, I wasn't hurt, but the bike was banged up pretty good. When I was still lying on the ground, I heard Benji make some smartass comment, and I jumped up to attack him. Slim got in the middle and tried to calm things down, though Benji was still adamant about not letting my accident slow him down. But it was too late for me. The fear was in me.

We were in the middle of nowhere, and despite my apprehension, I realized I had no choice but to get back on the bike. We agreed to try and find the highway together, so we could look for a hotel in

Siem Riep, but the problem was the front fork was bent, and I was so afraid of leaning into the turns that I had trouble keeping up. The feeling of going down was too fresh in my mind. It wasn't so much the idea of death as it was the fear of being mangled and left alive. I didn't like the idea of having no control over when the pain would end. I had seen enough of that with my dad.

After making our way to some run-down hotel, Benji went out to score some more smack. Although I was pretty pissed off with him, I was still amazed that no matter where he was, he always knew where to buy heroin. When he came back with the dope, I was tempted to take a shot—we were after all in the heart of the Golden Triangle, closer to the source than I'd probably ever be—but fortunately Benji had only one needle, and regardless of the temptation there was still no way I was about to share a rig with him.

Siem Riep was typical of most border towns. The vibe was rough, and no one there seemed like they particularly belonged. The people from Burma were part of the Shan tribe, wore sarongs, and had a noticeably different look from the Thai people. The only thing they had in common was a look of perpetual suspicion, criminality, and the quiet desperation of poverty. For years it had been one of the major distribution points for the international heroin trade, but now it seemed as if most of the dope business had been replaced with exporting huge amounts of Ya-Ba throughout Thailand and the rest of Asia.

***

The next morning, we crossed a bridge over the River Kwai into Burma. The border patrol looked over our passports with little scrutiny, and gave us a visa for the day. Aside from a small temple, there wasn't a whole lot happening on the Myanmar side. There was no real activity, commerce, or infrastructure—just a handful of small houses and huts that seemed stuck in some kind of never-ending waiting game. The only reason foreigners ever went there was to get their passports stamped in order to renew their Thai visas. Most people probably never even left the gate, just as I would do several times in the months ahead.

Later that day, Slim and Benji were itching to get back on the bikes and go out exploring. I knew I had to get back to Chiang Mai, but didn't feel like spending any more time on the bike than I needed to. Slim offered to ride back with me, but I didn't want to ruin their trip, so I told them to go ahead without me. I killed a little time walking around the town, but knew I was just prolonging the inevitable.

Eventually I got back on the bike and started the journey back to Chiang Mai. I figured that without having to keep up with anyone, I could take it slow and still make it back within a few hours. The problem was that the front tire was a little less than straight in the fork, and certain speeds seemed to amplify the wobble. Just as I figured out the right speed and awkward lean to keep a steady pace, it started to drizzle. The road became so slippery that it was already impossible to maintain traction, but it wasn't until it *really* started raining that the real misery began.

It's hard for people who have never been to Southeast Asia to imagine, but it was like a fucking tsunami: just sheets of water pouring down like the goddamned Niagara Falls. Just when it seemed it couldn't get any worse, my front brake cable (which was already kinked from the accident) suddenly snapped. The road was turning into a river, and I had to stay below ten miles an hour just to keep the tires grounded. Every time a car approached, I had to pull over to let it pass. And each time someone passed, a new wave of water came crashing down on me. I started alternating between crying to and cursing any and whatever god might hear my plight. I already had no helmet and couldn't see a fucking thing, so sure enough when the sun started to go down, the water fried my electrical system and my lights went out. That was when I just started praying for death.

At a few different points, I contemplated ditching the bike and hitching a ride, but I knew there would be serious repercussions. Not only did the bike-rental company have my credit card info, they also had a copy of my passport. Even though I was cold, soaking wet, and miserable, I had to keep going.

After hours of crawling down the road on a nearly unridable motorcycle—in the middle of nowhere, in complete darkness, during a torrential rainstorm—I saw a sign for a hotel. I got off the highway and started driving down some little road for almost an hour, until I was literally screaming for salvation. Right as I was about to turn around, which would have meant a two-hour detour for nothing, I saw someone wearing one of those Chinese straw hats that you see in old racist cartoons and Vietnam war movies—just standing there, in the rain, doing God knows what. He was only a poor farmer, but I imagined he was an angel that had been sent to save me. I asked him the best I could, in a broken combination of Thai and English, where the hotel was.

He smiled and looked at me like I was the craziest farang he had ever seen, and pointed to a narrow dirt path about twenty feet from where I was standing. If I hadn't seen him, I never would have stopped, and would have driven right by and missed the place entirely. There was no sign or anything, so I looked to him for reassurance, making sure he understood what I was asking, and then turned off into the mud. It was so deep I could barely push the bike through—but sure enough, about a hundred yards down, was a secluded building. I opened the door and hobbled in like some kind of wretched creature from the farang lagoon. I was soaking wet, totally covered in mud, and on the verge of a nervous breakdown, but I could instantly recognize that this was not just some cheap roadside motel. The inside was dimly lit, with accented vaulted ceilings, exotic hardwood paneling, and decorated with all kinds of plants, trees, and high-end artwork. The first person I saw was wearing a bathrobe, and finally I put it together that this wasn't a normal hotel at all...it was some kind of luxury health resort and spa. Definitely not the type of place where people normally just showed up to get off the road. But the Thai are kind people, especially to farangs, even dirty ones, just so long as they suspect you have a pocket full of cash. Sure enough, the rates for a room were ridiculous, but at that point we all knew I would be willing to pay literally any amount just to get out of the rain.

After they showed me to my room, I took off all my wet clothes and pulled out my sad little bag of dope, which of course was also soaked, and too wet to sniff. To think I had come so close to experiencing one fleeting moment of true comfort almost made me cry, but then I remembered the trick I had learned in Bangkok! My cigarette wrapper was already drenched, the foil peeled away from the paper just right...it all worked out perfectly. I smoked the rest of that shit in a few big hits, and had the best sleep of my life. The next morning, the sun was shining, and I made my way back to Chiang Mai.

***

Not long after Benji and Slim made it back to

the house, Benji again ran out of money. Knowing I wouldn't give him another fucking cent, he realized he had to head back to New York. A few days after he left, Slim realized I wasn't in the right mindset to try and put together a new band, so he left as well. He went up to a small town north of Chiang Mai called Pai, where he found a band to play gigs with in a small club. It was just me and Anne, and for the first time in my life, I had absolutely no direction and absolutely nothing to do. At first I tried to enjoy it. You get high, you fuck, you eat, and fuck again, but you can only do that for so long. We would go out for every meal. I'd take her shopping. We'd ride the scooter around town, and go to the Buddhist temples. I got some traditional Wai Khru tattoos, the kind they do with a stick while you say some prayers. More fucking, more dope. Repeat. But at a certain point, it just wasn't enough. It couldn't fill the void. The emptiness. After a few weeks, despite how hard I worked at trying to feel nothing, I was getting bored.

***

Sometime in the middle of November, I received an email from some friends in LA, who said they were coming to visit. They wanted to go to the beach at Ko Phi Phi. Anne and I were happy to get out of Chiang Mai, and flew out to meet them. Turquoise water, limestone cliffs. Beautiful.

We visited Slim up in Pai, a cool, hip little place, and found him by hearing his drumming the first night we got into town. The club was packed, and they were rocking out. He was happy. He wound up staying there for years, until he burned down a house in an opium-smoking accident. But for me, something wasn't right. Life was still going on, and I was just waiting for it to end. People were asking me if I'd ever come back to the States...if I was ever going to play music again. I didn't know the answer.

I had been talking to Karina in New York pretty frequently, and she had been planning to come meet us in Bangkok for Christmas. She knew all about Anne and was not only totally cool with the whole thing, but was actually looking forward to meeting her. Thankfully they each dug chicks, and of course I dug chicks who dug other chicks, so I was looking forward to things as well. I hadn't seen Karina since September 9th, two days before the whole world changed; and after picking her up at the airport we went to a hotel to catch up. She brought me some Christmas cookies that my mother had made. The same ones she had been making every year since 1964. But something was different. After spending a few hours with Karina, I figured it out.

I had an apartment in another part of Bangkok where Anne was waiting, so we set up a time to meet the next day. When Karina saw Anne, they both smiled, and instantly I could tell they liked each other. It was like introducing cats to one another: you don't quite know what will happen until it happens. Luckily, it was like magic. For the next few weeks, we did a lot of drugs and went out to the clubs, but mostly stayed in bed and fucked. There are so many possibilities with two women. It was a beautiful thing. When I went to bed that first night, with Anne in one arm, and Karina in the other, I felt something that I hadn't felt in ages. I felt almost happy. We spent Christmas and the New Year together, and had a great few weeks of debauchery. But not long after seeing Karina again, I quickly realized what was missing, what was wrong. I needed to get back to New York. I had to come to terms with the fact that things weren't just going to end. Even if the world was dying, it would take time—and somehow knowing that was the scariest part of all. I had to figure out a way to go on. I had to learn to live again.

I needed to clean up before going back to New York. At that point, I had a big enough habit that I couldn't have even made it back on the flight without getting sick—and since I'd heard that Benji was busted for selling dope to tourists in Chiang Mai, and sentenced to seven years in Bang Kwang—I knew I didn't want to be carrying anything on the plane. Slowly I started weaning myself off, and went through a week of horrendous withdrawals. You could buy Tylenol 3s with codeine over the counter in Thailand, so after getting through the worst of it, I started taking handfuls to ease the symptoms a bit. By the middle of the second week, I decided it was time.

However, when I got to the airport, I was scared to go home.

***

After landing in JFK, I caught a cab back to my apartment on Canal Street. As soon as the skyline came into view, I could see that something was missing. Although I had seen the footage a million times, it was different when I saw it with my own eyes. My heart ached. Even after being home for a few weeks, something still wasn't right. I felt different, like an outsider, as if my grief wasn't the same as everyone else's. Since I wasn't there the day it happened, I didn't share the common experience—and somehow, that made it hurt worse. I don't know what I expected, but for the first time in my life, I didn't know what I was doing there. It didn't feel like home anymore. I felt like a stranger, and I couldn't shake it. It was supposed to be a fresh start. It wasn't.

JAPAN

One day when I was still in elementary school, a new girl came into my class. Her name was Megumi. The teacher told us that she and her family were from Japan, and that they had moved to New York because of her father's job. I was probably only seven or eight years old, but I fell in love with her immediately. I can still remember the Japanese schoolgirl outfit that she was wearing, with her socks pulled up to her knees and her little white sneakers. That image probably seeded some of my perverted Asian fetishes and fantasies that developed later in life, but at that point it was all still very innocent. Even though Megumi didn't speak any English, we must have instinctively recognized our mutual outsider status because we hit it off instantly.

Not long after we became friends, I was invited over to her house for a "play date." Her mother answered the door, gave me a little bow, and politely directed me to take off my shoes. As soon as I stepped inside, I felt this overwhelming sense of serenity, almost like stepping into an empty church, and I was amazed at how different it felt from my own home. I noticed that they had very little furniture, and somehow the absence of clutter created its own energy that was subtle yet powerful.

Even though Megumi had a slightly pigeon-toed walk, she moved with such grace for a child that she appeared to float around the house like a ghost. She took me downstairs to a ping-pong table they had in the basement, nodded her head, and smiled at me in a way that insinuated she wanted me to play. I grabbed the paddle as if it were a battle axe, and she held hers like a pair of chopsticks, and then she proceeded to destroy me in a match that wasn't even remotely competitive. Realizing that I did not possess the necessary hand-eye coordination to maintain even the most basic back-and-forth volley with her, she decided to show me her Japanese comic books instead. Then she took out some notebooks, and we sat on the floor and drew pictures together for the rest of the time I spent at her house. Before I left, we had a snack of Japanese cookies that were similar to animal crackers, but in the same shapes as the characters in her comic books.

As I was leaving, her mother gave me a box of the cookies to take with me. Although I never opened it, I kept that box for years...and would occasionally stare at it and imagine that if I could ever translate its symbols, I would discover some deep meaning that would somehow reveal the mysteries of her culture. Even though we never really spoke on that first visit, in just a few hours I learned that there was a whole universe that existed outside of my own small world—and that one day I would explore it.

I think it was a combination of my experiences with her, and my obsession with ninjas, that led to my specific interest in Japanese culture. I'd always been impressed with their concepts of beauty, and the mechanics behind their creation. I have always found the whole aesthetic very appealing. Even as a kid, I could recognize that there was some fundamental difference in their way of thinking and their general approach to life. How someone can take the time to put such care into arranging something as sparse as a rock garden is still beyond my comprehension, but their focus and dedication to whatever it is they are doing—and the attention they expend on the minute details while doing it—can seem mysterious to the average Westerner. In spite of this, I believed when I finally got to Japan, I would somehow break the code.

I was wrong.

Despite always being fascinated with Japan, actually going there was pretty much a spur-of-the-moment decision. I was on my way home from Thailand, on another layover in Tokyo, when I finally decided I should actually leave the airport. It was June of 2002, and I was still finding it impossible to get on with my life in New York. I suspected it could be my last time seeing Anne for a while though, and was hoping to get a new perspective on things. I had pretty much accepted that even if the planet was gonna keep on spinning, the world would always have its series of disasters. The time had come for me to try and focus once again—even if I couldn't be a warrior, or the savior of the world, I needed to figure out a way to master my own mind. Since I'd read a lot about the concepts of Zen and of having One Mind, that day seemed as good as any to explore the possibility.

***

I left Narita Airport for a hotel, and somehow managed to navigate my way through the subway system. As soon as I stepped out of the station at Shibuya, I was immediately engulfed in a frenetic metropolitan energy that I had rarely found anywhere outside New York.

I knew beforehand that everything in Tokyo was going to be expensive, so I wasn't surprised to find that my room was smaller than a typical jail cell. The only reason the room was even available was because someone had just cancelled their reservation. Despite the lack of space, everything was so neat, clean, and well-organized that it was actually quite comfortable. After washing my face, I dropped off my bags and decided to head back outside to check out the scene. After a short walk, I found myself in Shibuya Crossing, which is kinda like the Japanese version of Times Square. Tons of people walking in every direction, and huge neon signs everywhere. There is also a statue of a dog called Hachiko, who after his owner died, waited every day for nine years at the train station where they normally met after work. Same spot, same time, he waited and waited, even though the man never showed up. Apparently even Japanese dogs set a high standard for themselves!

Later that night, I somehow wound up in Roppongi, which seemed to be the hangout for all the other *gaijin* like me. There seemed to be a lot of them, but I hadn't yet put the pieces together as to *why* there were so many. I went into a bar and started drinking heavily. The prices were ridiculous, but I didn't care. I was drinking vodka and beer, trying to cover up a slight junk sickness, and was getting wasted very quickly.

I don't know how true the stories were, or how often it actually happened, but apparently the area was notorious for people's drinks being spiked. Now I can't say for sure that it happened to me, but I was definitely wasted in a way that was not normal. Even so, if someone thought they would knock me out and rob me, they wasted their pill.

The next few hours became a blur of bright lights, pachinko parlors, and drunken stupidity. I vaguely remember making the rounds with some Russian models I had met at the bar, but I can't say anything for sure. By the time I saw the sun coming up, I knew it was time to call it a night. I could barely stand, and the morning traffic was already starting to congest the streets. Incredibly, I made it back to the hotel and stumbled my way through the lobby. When I finally got back into the room, the walls spun until I passed out.

***

When I woke up that afternoon, the first thing I noticed was that I was wet. Very wet. My skull was pounding, and my first thought was that I must have spilled something on myself in my drunken stupor. I looked around and realized there were no empty bottles or knocked-over drinks...something much worse had occurred. I had pissed in the goddamned bed.

I felt like the biggest fucking degenerate on earth. Here I was, halfway around the planet, in a country filled with some of the most self-disciplined and honorable people in the world, lying in a puddle of my own fucking piss. Sure, the room was small for almost 30,000 yen a night, but nothing warranted me pissing in their fucking bed! What would Megumi say if she could see me now? Dope never made me behave this way. I decided that maybe this was why there were no good white ninjas.

As hard as I tried to remember what had happened, I couldn't. I tried to tell myself that maybe I really was drugged, but knew I was just trying to come up with some poor excuse for my behavior. And besides, I doubted anyone would really want to waste any Rohypnol on me. I had to accept that I was just a fucking mess.

To make matters worse, someone was knocking on the door. I looked through the peephole and saw the cleaning lady. As much as I wanted my room to return to its pristine former glory, I was too ashamed to let her in. In my still half-drunk state, I decided to ignore her, and hoped the whole situation would somehow dissipate like a bad dream. But, of course, it didn't. How do you clean a piss-soaked bed anyway?

I jumped in the shower, put on some fresh clothes, and headed out to find some water and aspirin. As I was leaving the hotel, the lady at the front desk asked if I needed the cleaning service to make up my room—as if they knew I was guilty of something heinous. I politely refused, thanked her, and bowed in an attempt to cover up my white shame.

I found a place to shovel down some food, but despite eating a handful of Tylenol, just couldn't shake the headache or creeping dope sickness. I decided to have a drink, and ordered a shot of whiskey. That seemed to help, so I ordered a few more and began a repeat of the previous night. After I finished pounding down my fourth or fifth, a mob of drunken Irish hooligans walked into the bar with obnoxious green plastic horns and stupid oversized leprechaun hats. In under a minute, I was surrounded by them. Judging from the fact that most were wearing jerseys, it was obvious they were in town for some kind of soccer match. Suddenly, the huge crowds of foreigners that had been fucking everywhere since the minute I stepped off the plane all began making sense. Jesus Christ. Short of when the nuclear bombs were dropped on Hiroshima and Nagasaki, I couldn't have picked a worse time to visit Japan. It was the goddamned World Cup.

One of the maniacs began grabbing my arm and started yelling something into my ear. Another one asked me if I was Irish, and while I knew I was probably throwing away a few free drinks by denying it, and despite actually being part Irish, I lied and said I wasn't. My Italian father would occasionally break my balls about being part Irish, and by the looks of this crowd, I could see his point. I didn't know anything about soccer, and I really didn't want to be associated with any of these "football" fanatics, but I knew my chance of that would almost certainly be in vain. *We* probably all looked the same to the Japanese anyway. Drunken European mobs, beds being pissed in... Oh my God, I was one of them. I was part of the problem. I was the reason for Sokoku, the Japanese isolation that didn't allow foreigners into their country until the mid-nineteenth century. White people were a scourge on common decency—and I, too, was a leper.

I had to get out of there. I knew I would be seen as a target, looked upon with disgust, while simultaneously being overcharged on every single consumable item. This wasn't what I had come to Japan for. I knew I had to get out of the area, possibly even out of Tokyo, but once again I was drunk, and instead was convinced by somebody to go to another nearby club called Gaspanic.

On the walk over, I discovered my new acquaintance wasn't Irish, but Portuguese. It turned out he had moved to Tokyo a few years earlier with his parents, who owned some kind of clothing company. He kept getting calls on his cell phone, but it was obvious he wasn't discussing anything garment-related. I could tell by his threads that he was a raver, and I assumed he was selling club drugs.

When we got to the door, they must have recognized him because they let the two of us in without charging the ridiculously high covers they were asking. As soon as we got inside, he told me that he had some deals lined up to sell Ecstasy. He claimed to have some connection in Ibiza who shipped him the pills at a low price: since drugs were scarce in Tokyo, he got away with charging exuberant amounts, in excess of $100 a hit. He asked me if I wanted one, but I told him that at that price I would have to pass. He handed me one anyway and said it was on him. I popped it in my mouth and thanked him.

Apparently, even the bartenders liked my new friend because they were giving both of us free drinks while we sat at the bar. Every ten minutes or so, he would run off to conduct his business and, by the third or fourth time, I started feeling the E. I decided to walk over to the main dance floor, and saw that the place was filled with young Japanese kids, and American GIs on R&R. The pulsing house beat was starting to grate at my nerves, and even though I was only twenty-six at the time, I was starting to feel like a claustrophobic old man. I had to escape.

I found my drug-dealing friend as I was headed out the door, and told him I just couldn't handle the whole vibe of the joint and had to split. Before I left, I asked him if he knew any places that might have some live music, and he directed me to a club on the opposite end of town that was popular with the local bands. I thanked him for his generosity and got the hell out of there.

Outside, I considered taking the subway across town, but decided there was no way that I would make it in my condition. Instead, I waved down a taxi and told the driver to take me to a club called Milk. There was traffic everywhere, and by the time I made it inside the venue, the show was already over. I found out the rock shows ended early, so people could get home before the train system shut down.

I was drunk as hell, high on Ecstasy, and trying to figure out my next move when I spotted some blond chick sitting alone on the curb outside the club. As soon as I looked at her, she stood up and walked over to introduce herself. She was English and apparently in town for the World Cup—like me, she was not the slightest bit interested in football, but tagged along with her friends for the chance to visit Tokyo. We talked about music for a minute, and then she asked me where I was staying. She told me some nonsense about not wanting to go back and disturb her friends, and basically said she was going back to my room with me.

It normally wasn't my style to hook up like that, but in my drunken state I jumped into a taxi with her and we started fooling around. She wasn't the Japanese schoolgirl of my fantasies, but in the state I was in, I couldn't really complain. By the time we made it back to Shibuya, my dick felt like it had been hooked up to a car battery, and I was starting to hit my peak on the E. But right as we were pulling up to the front of the hotel, I suddenly remembered my "accident." I had put it out of my mind all day, and now it was coming back to haunt me like a sledgehammer to the groin. I tried to think up some excuse for why she couldn't come up to my room, and made up some bullshit about having to catch a flight early in the morning. She looked at me like I was insane. When she realized that I was actually being serious, she gave me a look that said I was the biggest piece of shit she had ever seen. I handed the driver enough money to take her wherever she needed to go, apologized profusely, and jumped out of the cab.

***

When I got back inside my room, I realized my entire trip was a failure. I tried to find a comfortable position on the floor, but the room was so small there was hardly any place to sit, let alone lie down. I considered trying to find another hotel, but I knew rooms were scarce because of the World Cup, and in my current state it would probably be useless anyway. Everything was useless. I hadn't broken the secret code of the Japanese ninjas that I'd been trying to discover

since I was a kid. I had no more insight into the beauty, the grace, or the honor of the Japanese people than I had before I got there. I hadn't even really spoken to any Japanese people since landing in the country. I hadn't discovered the focus, the clarity, or the discipline required to achieve a Zen state, or a quiet "one" mind. I was too busy trying to figure out how to arrange empty bottles of water to make it look like I'd accidentally spilled a few liters into the dead center of the bed (in the hope that I wouldn't be charged some outrageous fee by the hotel for destroying their property). I was a loser, and I had to resign myself to my shame.

I decided I needed to punish myself, and that I should lie back down in the bed of my own making, a bed soaked with my own piss. I just wanted to die. And finally I realized that was the only answer—it had been right in front of me the whole time! I remembered reading about the concept of Haji, or immense shame, and suddenly everything became clear. The only thing for me to do to preserve my honor would be to commit suicide, to perform hara-kiri. I looked around for something to cut my own guts out with, but the only utensil I found was a dirty pair of chopsticks. I considered going back outside to see if I could find a place that sold samurai swords, but I was covered in piss and too drunk to clean myself up. I couldn't even commit suicide with honor.

And at the heart of it, this was the major difference between our two cultures—we have a much higher threshold for shame. We can make immense assholes of ourselves, embarrass ourselves to no end, and somehow manage to let it go and brush it all off. I was an ugly American dammit, and maybe it was just time for me to go home once and for all.

***

It was early dawn. The pachinko parlors were closed, and there were still a few minutes before the trains started running. On my walk down the stairs into the subway station, I passed a few Japanese businessmen in suits, passed out on the ground like bums. After seeing that one of them had a large wet spot around his crotch, it finally hit me. It didn't make me feel any better about my own degeneracy; it was the fact that we all needed to accept that the times are changing, and that maybe we aren't so different after all. Maybe everyone was struggling to find their place in this new world. Maybe the traditions of the past hadn't equipped anyone with the necessary tools to navigate our new reality. The uncertainty of life, the filth, had spread across the entire globe. No one was immune. I realized I could spend the rest of my life traveling around the world and still never find any answers. At the end of the day, there were no mystical boxes of cookies. We are all just people...some of us may be a little higher than others, but all still struggling to find our place.

NEW YORK

For years after having my first psychedelic experience, I tried to recapture the beauty, the mystery, and the insight of my first few trips. Since my early teens, I'd tried nearly every psychoactive substance that I could get my hands on, always in an attempt to receive what I can only describe as some kind of a communion. I believed that through achieving a heightened state of consciousness, I might somehow be able to experience that thing that most of us can only refer to as God. I had seen just enough to be convinced that there was something else out there, something bigger than us all. There had to be. Whether that thing was actually somewhere "out there," or within us, I wasn't so sure. What I did know was that each time I opened those doors of perception, I was also leaving myself vulnerable to a whole lot of bad shit. That was a problem for me. I didn't need any more bad shit. At that point, I just wanted to lock the joint up and close myself off to everything.

When I got back to New York, I tried

desperately to find my place again. I could see that most people were starting to get back into their routines, going to work, shopping for groceries, doing the laundry—but, for the life of me, I just couldn't get on with it. After traveling all over the world in search of answers, I felt like I knew even less than when I had first moved into the city ten years earlier. All I knew was that I was tired. I didn't want to search for answers; I just wanted to find a little peace of mind...I wanted to be happy.

Months went by where I barely left my apartment. I was becoming a complete and total hermit. There were days when I didn't even bother to get out of bed. But one day, for some reason that I can't even remember, I had to stop off at a friend's place on First Avenue. The apartment had been around for years, and always had a steady rotation of NYU students and club kids who'd lived there since the early nineties. That day, I ran into a girl named Cloüd, who I had hooked up with acid and mushrooms a few times many years earlier. She started telling me all about how she had been cultivating her own natural psychedelics— like San Pedro and peyote, and told me that she had even begun brewing her own ayahuasca. After showing me a few of her homemade concoctions, she started giggling like a witch and told me that she had recently acquired something really special.

I had tried DMT years earlier but with relatively unsuccessful results. I remembered feeling a little something and had experienced some mild visuals, but these had passed very quickly and were altogether unremarkable. I knew that DMT had a reputation for being extremely powerful stuff, and wasn't sure if my initial experience was because I'd had too small a dose, if I had smoked it wrong, or if the quality was just subpar. Either way, she insisted I had to try it again, and that I should do it right then and there. I tried to explain that my head had been in a pretty bad place, and that I certainly wasn't planning on taking any trips that day…but she was persistent, and convinced me that this was even more of a reason why it was a good time to take it. Besides, she said it would only take a few minutes.

Over the years, I had become a little apprehensive about entheogens, especially without good reason to believe it was high-quality stuff. But she swore that it was made by a chemist of the highest order, and that it was as pure as a newborn's soul. When I finally, and somewhat reluctantly, agreed, she started giggling again as she prepared my dose. As she did, her eyes were bugging out of her head, and there was a big grin on her face—as if she was about to let me in on some big secret. Like everything else had been mere child's play. This, she said, would blow my mind.

She began by packing some hand-blown glass with a piece of a mushroom cap. I'd never seen anyone do that before, and had never heard of anyone smoking mushrooms, but I figured she knew what she was doing. She then scooped a small spoonful of white powder on top and handed me the pipe. She insisted I sit down on the edge of her bed, and she held up a flame from a lighter, just barely touching her concoction. As I was inhaling this foul-smelling smoke, she encouraged me not to stop until I couldn't inhale anymore. When I was out of breath, she told me to hold it in as long as I could. The smoke tasted terrible, like burnt mothballs. As I was holding the hit in my lungs, I looked up and saw that she had a huge smile on her face. Before I even finished exhaling, I fell back onto the bed.

She must have put on some electronic trance music because suddenly I heard this beat in a way that I had never heard or felt before. Within an instant, the room was transformed into what appeared to be some kind of spaceship. As soon as I realized what I was looking at, I thought, *Oh my God, I am being abducted by aliens.* It seemed like my whole body was enveloped in a strange light; colors more vivid and bright than anything I'd ever seen. I don't remember if my eyes were open or closed, but it didn't matter—the place I was in transcended all aspects of the physical plane...like some kind of psychic mothership. And I knew that I was not alone...that I was somehow in the presence of a highly evolved entity. Whatever it was, this was first contact. But I was not afraid. I was beyond fear.

Time seemed to have no relevance and space seemed infinite. It felt like I had gone beyond the confines of my physical self, as if having an out-of-body experience. I remember looking down at myself lying there on the bed. I knew it was my body, but it was not me. And then suddenly my perspective changed again, and I felt like I had become one with some benevolent form of energy, traveling through the universe at the speed of light. I realized that there was nothing just "out there" or "in me"—it was everywhere, in the macro and the micro. Simultaneously, in every dimension, the cosmic stardust that created the universe, this creative force, was everywhere, and was everything...all at once. And it was aware. It was *alive*.

And just as I was trying to comprehend the enormity of this new and simple truth, a suddenly obvious fact dawned on me—that we are all connected—and for a moment I experienced a fleeting sense of comfort. But before I had a chance to savor it, I felt it all begin to slip away. Not long after having this tremendous realization, I was returned to my body and started to see things with my own eyes once again. I looked around and noticed I was back in the mothership, and felt as if something was looking down at me...smiling. I wondered if these were the angels and spirits, the gnomes and elves, the extraterrestrials and aliens that I had communicated with before—around us, and within us, all of the time, but always just out of reach. And then I was again engulfed in light, and felt as if I was being returned to our normal plane of existence. I could hear my heart beating, merging into the beat of the trance music; and as my usual auditory perception started to return, I had the sense that I had been transported back from a portal, returned into my regular state of being. As I was starting to feel my body, the room began to take on its physical properties once again. Then, just as quickly as it began, it was over.

***

It took me a minute to remember where I was, and what had happened. Just as I could feel my neural circuits re-establishing their usual pathways, I looked up and saw Cloüd staring at me with a big grin on her face. I sat up slowly and desperately tried to put everything into perspective. Cloüd asked or said something along the lines of, "So, how was it?" but I couldn't yet put the words together. Besides, I knew she already knew the answer. When I was finally able to communicate, I asked how long I had been "gone" for. Although I had seemingly traveled beyond the limits of time and space, apparently less than ten minutes had actually passed.

I couldn't believe so much had happened in such a short period of time. As hard as I tried to make sense of everything, I realized there would never be any tangible way to quantify the experience. The only thing I knew…was that there was no way to diminish its implications. If our minds were capable of functioning in this capacity, whatever had occurred could not simply be dismissed as a mere chemical reaction. The DMT itself was nothing more than a tool…a way to access knowledge...something both ancient and futuristic, existing within the knowledge gaps between astrophysics and religion. I tried to imagine what people much smarter than myself could learn from it, but became overwhelmed by the enormity of it all. And even if these experiences were still just a small part of our collective consciousness, I knew that somehow they would play a part in our evolution as a species. And while I still had no idea what I was supposed to do with this new information...for one fleeting moment it didn't seem to matter. All that mattered was that there was a reason for it...that it meant something.

***

For years and years, I had tried to get to a certain point...the trip to end all trips. When it hit me that I had finally gotten a glimpse into our ultimate destiny, it turned out to be so much more than anything I could have ever imagined...a new horizon that aside from a small group of misfits and psychonauts had been left largely unexplored. Even if the physical world was exactly as I'd left it, the true reality of our existence now seemed completely different. Somehow it didn't really matter if the world was coming to an end...because I finally understood that nothing ever really ends—it just changes. Even a full-on planetary apocalypse would be little more than a transition into a different reality. No matter how sick the Earth was, or how shitty it would be to not survive, something told me when the time finally came, I would know what to do.

THE SOUTH

In 2006, I turned thirty years old and decided it was time to leave New York. The expiration date I had given myself to become a rock star had passed, and I knew the time had finally come to pack it in. All of the lifestyle choices I had been making for half my life had not achieved the desired, and perhaps even expected, results. I was not notorious, a millionaire, or dead. Never leaving myself with a contingency plan in case my career didn't work out was intentional; the fact that I was still alive was not. Nevertheless, there I was, still breathing. If I was going to keep on living, I knew I would somehow have to come up with a new plan. Merely surviving couldn't cut it anymore.

The truth was, the writing had been on the wall for some time. Even aside from my own failure to reconcile the role of an artist with managing and maintaining the business end of the music industry, it was all going to shit anyway. At the same time that things really started to fall apart with my band and my contacts in the industry, online file-sharing programs were showing the record-buying public that there were ways to acquire music without actually having to pay for it. Everything I had done up until that point had been a means to an end, but it was no longer clear to me, and to many musicians, what that end even was anymore. Regardless, before I called it quits, before I could fully turn my back on all of the mythology and kill the dream once and for all, I knew I had to go to the source of all my original aspirations, ambitions, and delusions, and somehow figure out a way to reverse-engineer my psychosis. So I rented an RV and headed south for Clarksville, Mississippi.

The intersection of Highways 61 and 49 is the crossroads. The actual and literal place where Robert Johnson supposedly made a deal with the devil...and where all of the folklore that defined what it meant to be successful in rock-and-roll began. But aside from an old gas station and a couple of fried-chicken joints, there was nothing really there. I waited around for a while to see if there might be any last-minute bids for my soul, but no one showed up.

After that, I drove over to Hopson Plantation to figure out whether it had all been worth it for Mr. Johnson, but it was hard to get a clear answer. That his life came to a dark end was indisputable, but the question still remained: was it really *worth* it? He died young, long before legions of aspiring guitarists and blues enthusiasts began devouring all the little nuances of his limited body of work. Was it possible that he somehow knew that one day he would become a legend and make a huge dent in the history of recorded music? And even if so, would he have happily traded his life for that knowledge? I didn't yet know. If there was any chance of me getting past the idea that life could mean more than the legacy we leave behind, I knew I would need to turn something around. Both metaphorically and physically. So I got back in the RV and headed north toward Memphis.

***

Graceland, in the long and fabled story of rock-and-roll, was supposed to exemplify all the pinnacles of success. Despite the arguments some could make that he was nothing more than an imposter, there was no denying the impact made by Elvis. The proof was in the lines of people from around the world all hoping to get some small glimpse of what could turn a truck driver into the King. But again, just like with Robert Johnson, the end result was the same. The only difference was unlike the King of the Delta Blues, there was none of the same mystery surrounding the conclusion of Elvis's story. All you have to do is look at a few pictures from his last days and it quickly becomes obvious that he was a sad, lonely, and miserable son of a bitch. That there was a pattern was becoming more and more clear. It wasn't just my imagination—Sun Studios, Beale Street, Stax…it was all the same. The glory had passed. It wasn't just because the icons had died; the spirit was gone as well.

***

Somewhere on the ride east toward Nashville, the drugs ran out. I didn't need to make it all the way to the Grand Ol' Opry to contemplate how another one of my heroes' lives had ended. The demise of Hank Sr. was better documented than just about anyone's. Everyone knew Hank would kick the bucket early, well before they found his stiff corpse in the back of a blue Cadillac on New Year's Day. So I pulled the RV into a campground and decided to start detoxing in a place where I knew I wouldn't be able to find any dope, no matter how hard I tried. I parked deep enough into the woods that regardless of how loud I screamed, no one would hear my agony. For over a week, I went through some of the worst withdrawals of my life. Days on end without sleep, soaking wet from sweat and various other bodily fluids. I kicked and thrashed in that RV like a caged animal, until one morning I heard birds chirping and howling and making a commotion the likes of which I'd never heard. And it was beautiful. As the sun slowly started to rise, I knew the worst was behind me.

When it was all over, I was able to see things more clearly. None of the usual haze and fog I was used to. Everything was so crisp and in focus that it seemed like I could see the world with laser precision. And that scared the shit out of me. Because I knew once I got out of those woods, I would again have to face the reality that so much of the world really sucked. But I had made a deal with myself, and ultimately there were no other options left. I had to try and figure out a new way.

I got an apartment in Nashville and over the next few months, more and more of my old life started to change. The game in Nashville was totally different than in New York and Los Angeles. It seemed that the musicians there were somehow allowed to grow older, without having their entire self-worth measured exclusively in fame. I bought a pair of cowboy boots and tried desperately to wash away the stigma of my old life. Nobody knew anything about me or my past, and for a while that suited me just fine. I mainly hung out in a honky-tonk called Robert's Western World, and drank my ass off almost every waking moment. I didn't have any connection for opiates, and I didn't look, but there always seemed to be some cocaine around, and I did as much as I could get my hands on. I was socializing more than I ever had in my whole life. Making the rounds with people who for the most part knew nothing about me beyond this new character I had created. There were moments when even I would almost forget who I'd once been.

Eventually the novelty of being a tourist in a new town began to wear off, and the realities and stresses of day-to-day life set in. My relationship with Karina was getting worse by the day. Our marriage had already been on the rocks before we left New York, and it didn't take long before all of our old problems began to resurface. To make matters worse, she didn't like Hank Williams or cowboy boots AT ALL. It turned out that she was even less crazy about my new persona than the maniac she had been with for over a decade, and sure enough, when it all finally ended, it ended badly.

It took some time, but once I managed to get through the initial self-pity and depression, the partying resumed with a renewed sense of vengeance and reckless abandon. I still managed to stay off the dope, but even that couldn't negate the fact that my self-destructive tendencies were accelerating at a more pronounced rate than ever before. One morning after an especially brutal three-day-long bender, it became obvious, even to me, that I was reaching my breaking point. I had been hitting it hard with my friend Zach, who played upright bass with a few of the bands on Lower Broadway. We had a lot in common: we were both northern transplants with a shared affinity for classic country music; we were both going through nasty divorces; and we both had insatiable appetites for drinking, drugs, and debauchery. When no one else could go the distance, I could always count on Zach to be a great partner for the most depraved affairs. But that morning, there was no denying we were both on our last legs.

We decided we needed to get out of town for a little bit, and since we were both broke as shit, tried to come up with a plan that required little or no money. With bleary eyes and a crusty nose,

Zach mentioned that he knew a guy in South Carolina with a few cabins he thought we could use for free—and after making a quick phone call, confirmed we were good to go. Since we hadn't slept for three days, we passed out for a few hours and then hit the road.

To get geared up, we each took a few key blasts of coke and headed to the gas station to fill up the tank of my decrepit Jeep Cherokee. Since there was no stereo, we picked up a cheap boom box, threw on some Roger Miller, and jumped on the interstate. For hours, Zach schooled me on the terminology and etiquette required to maintain proper CB communications. As far as I knew, he didn't own a ham radio, but perhaps on account of his extensive viewing of the *Smokey and the Bandit* series, he made some pretty convincing arguments for himself. Six hours later, we managed to make it to a small town outside Spartanburg, South Carolina—relieved we had made it the whole way without the floorboards catching fire.

***

When we pulled up to the farm, we were greeted by a man who looked like he had just stepped out of central casting. He was of an indeterminate middle age, probably not as old as he looked, was barefooted, wore dirty overalls, and had a gray beard down to the middle of his chest. He was wearing a felt hat that looked like it may have been a fedora at one time, and to top it all off, he had a live possum sitting on his shoulder. Zach introduced the man as Barney Farmwell, and I was told he was a moonshiner. The possum, I learned, was named George Jones.

The whole scene was just too fucking much. I had traveled all over the world, always hoping for a chance to make contact with some rare indigenous culture, and here I was, in the United States, face-to-face with a man who looked like some prospector who'd headed into the wild back in the 1800s and never came back out. I couldn't fucking believe it. I seriously didn't even know people like him existed anymore, but, sure enough, there he was, one of the last of his kind.

***

He invited us into his house and poured us each a drink of some strawberry-infused moonshine. It turned out his wife was out of town, and that we'd come at a good time. He had a few instruments lying around and Confederate flags and memorabilia all over the place. It was obvious he took pride in being a real southern outlaw, but in a way that wasn't some kind of closed-minded redneck cliché. He was a hillbilly for sure, but smart and generous as hell. He told us that he had come from a long line of moonshiners, and although you could tell he capitalized on his persona, it was obvious it wasn't some act. He was the real deal. To thank him for his generosity, we busted out the last of our blow and did rails off his wooden table—getting shit-faced together and talking music and politics for hours.

When the sun started coming up, he took us out to show us the land that had been in his family for generations. About twenty years earlier, he had begun hosting a bluegrass festival on the property and wound up building a few extra cabins out back. Before we crashed, he pulled out a Mason jar of his private reserve. I don't know what that shit was, but after a few sips I got more wasted than I'd ever been in my life. I was already drunk as hell, but after that, I couldn't even figure out which direction the ground was. While I stumbled to get inside one of the cabin doors, I was warned that while I could sleep wherever I liked, one of the rooms was reserved for George Jones…who he said liked to bite.

It was sometime in the afternoon when I woke up in the stifling heat with a motherfucker of a headache. I found Zach a few doors down, in just as bad shape as me. Each cabin was themed with a different southern state, and decorated with Barney's chainsaw art to give a more delicate, and personal, touch. I think Zach was in Texas. When we were finally able to pull it together to head out for some food, we found Barney stark naked in a creek behind the cabins. He was videotaping himself for a movie he claimed to be making about moonshining. How exactly bathing nude fit into it, I still don't know. I've never seen the film.

***

When we got back, Barney told us he had to run off for a while to take care of some business, and me and Zach started up a fire to grill some of the meat we'd picked up. Suddenly, we heard something that sounded like a bomb had gone off. We looked in the direction of the explosion, a few hundred yards away, and saw a huge plume of smoke coming up over the tree line. We ran down one of the trails that cut through the woods, until we came up on an old motor home engulfed in flames. A minute later, Barney ran up, wide-eyed but surprisingly calm. Not sure what the hell had happened, we asked what we could do to help, but he said we needed to stay clear because there was going to be another explosion any second. We could hear a hissing sound, as if someone had opened up a pressure valve. Sure enough, less than a minute later, there was another tremendous boom, so loud it hurt my ears. Flames were shooting up sixty feet into the sky, and smoke was pumping out of it like a locomotive. Barney admitted he had one of his stills in that camper, and something had obviously gone very wrong. We asked if this sort of thing happened often, and he said it never had before. If he had been inside when that still went off, he would have been toast.

He grabbed a hose in a halfhearted attempt to spray down the flames, but we all knew there was no way to extinguish it. For a moment, we just stood there like idiots, totally entranced, but within a minute realized the smoke would be seen for miles, and Barney knew he'd be having some more visitors soon. He told us if we wanted to help, we needed to follow him down one of the paths that led to a small shed. Inside were a couple of fifty-five-gallon drums filled with White Lightning. He asked us to move them deep into the woods and cover them up the best we could with leaves and tree branches. Just as we were finishing trying to camouflage them, we heard the first sirens.

When the first fire truck pulled onto his property, it had no way to get to the actual fire. Barney must have known some of the local firemen because they were joking around as everyone stood watching the mobile home burn. Within a few minutes, another fire truck showed up, as well as a few police cars. After about forty-five minutes, the feds showed up and, by that point, no one was joking around. It seemed that no matter what I did, or where I went, I couldn't get away from the insanity.

They split us up and started asking us all kinds of questions. I answered truthfully that me and Zach were just a couple of musicians visiting from Nashville, who really had no idea what was going on. Barney told them that he had just created a mockup of a still to make a movie about how people *used* to make moonshine. I saw him showing the feds his beat-up old VHS camera like it was some high-tech piece of movie-making equipment, but it was hard to tell if they were buying any of it. He was such a character, even by South Carolina standards, that I think they just didn't know what to make of it all. In one last-ditch attempt to prove that this was all just "showbiz," he said, "Hey! I been telling these here fellers that you boys was just in town to work on some music for the movie with me, and well...they just wanna hear us play a song 'er two fer 'em!" Me and Zach didn't even bat an eye before we said sure and ran over to the cabins to grab our instruments.

We had never played anything together, but we knew we had to somehow repay Barney for his hospitality. After over an hour of questioning, the moonshine still continued to burn bright into the night, and Barney ran back to us with an old fiddle. In front of about a dozen different firemen, police officers, and ATF agents all standing around with their arms crossed, looking skeptical as all hell, Barney whispered to us, "You boys know the 'Orange Blossom Special'?"

Less than a year after moving south of the Mason-Dixon line, resigned to the fact that it was time to quit playing music altogether, I found myself chugging away on an open E chord with more urgency than I'd ever had in my whole life— until the old moonshiner finally shouted out: "Look yonder comin'!"

After a few minutes of Barney improvising the intro, complete with train sounds and chicken and pig noises, we went into the double-time breakdown, and I could see the feds were starting to lighten up. When they began bobbing their heads, tapping their toes, and smiling, I knew that we had somehow managed to keep Barney out of jail, at least for the night.

After we finished the song, the fire finally started to die down, and the firemen, cops, and feds all started to leave, one by one. Barney didn't have to say anything, but he did mumble something about the fact that we were "all right for a couple of Yankees."

***

When I got back to Nashville, I was shot. I knew it was time to make some serious changes, but couldn't seem to find much of an incentive. I looked around, but couldn't find a purpose, a reason to hold it all together. But then, just when I assumed my heart was too dark to ever allow myself to feel much of anything again, I met Darlin'. She was a tiny little thing, but a real beauty, and tough as nails. It took a little time to convince her I could get my act together, but when I finally did, it became obvious that we were starting to dig each other pretty hard. Over the next few months, I began breaking some of my bad habits. I cut down on the booze and coke, started working a "real" job for the first time since I was sixteen, and finalized my divorce. But just in case I wasn't turning my life around quickly enough, one day I got some news that imparted a whole new level of urgency. I found out I was going to become a father.

AFRICA

Not long after getting together with Darlin', I let her cut my hair. I'd had long hair since I was in my early teens, and it was very much a part of my identity—the very identity I was determined to destroy. In some kind of weird Sampson and Delilah act, she pulled my hair into a ponytail, grabbed a pair of scissors, and in one snip took away all of the power and insanity that I had somehow always associated with my youth. It was at that moment, while staring down at that long pile of hair, that I believe I started to become an adult. I quit traveling, playing music, and using drugs. For the first time in my life, I actually began to settle down. Over the next few years, we wound up having two beautiful kids—I started up a successful business, and bought a nice home in a good school district. The ten years that passed since I had moved to Tennessee went by in the blink of an eye.

***

In the spring of 2016, a few weeks after I turned forty, we decided to take a road trip up to New York to see my family. We dropped off the pets at the kennel, packed up my new Jeep Wrangler (that didn't have a tendency to catch fire), and headed toward the Northeast. Since my kids were still little, we took it slow, and made lots of stops. We stayed in four- and five-star hotels along the way, and stopped off in Philly and DC to see the sites. After a few days, we made it to my sister's house in Long Beach, where we met up with my mother. Her sixty-fifth birthday was coming up, and me and my sister had decided we were going to take her on a safari. I hadn't traveled outside of the States since moving to Tennessee, and although my passport had long since expired, I'd always wanted to see some animals in Africa before they all went extinct.

***

That first night, my sister wanted to go see a Grateful Dead cover band that was playing at one of the local bars. I had never been a fan of the Dead, and for years had ragged on her for being into all that hippie shit—but aside from doing a little business outside of a few Dead shows in the early nineties, I thought the whole scene was a drag. Despite all of this, I had nothing better to do, and wasn't going to pass up the rare opportunity to get out and take advantage of the fact that my mom was around to babysit. On the ride over to the club, my sister broke out a little glass pipe and started packing it up with some weed. Even though it had been over ten years since I'd last smoked pot, I would have recognized that smell anywhere—it was the real-deal Sour Diesel. I didn't even know that the strain was still around, but apparently my sister was tied in with some of the serious stoners who made sure it had never really gone away. She passed me the pipe and, after getting a little side-glanced look from Darlin', I took a hit.

The club was filled with middle-aged Dead Heads, who all seemed to know my sister. I was being introduced to all these new people, who were coming up and giving me hugs like long-lost family members. Not long after ordering a round of drinks, the band started tuning up. Once they started playing, most of the crowd made their way up to the stage and started bobbing their heads. Everyone seemed to know everyone else, and everyone knew the songs, and it didn't take long before almost everyone was dancing.

I was already feeling pretty stoned when one of my sister's friends walked over and handed me some kind of vaporizer filled with a concentrate of liquid THC. To be polite, I took a hit and within seconds the room started spinning. I hadn't smoked weed in so long that it started to feel like the first time I'd gotten stoned as a kid. Suddenly the band started to go into some heavy psychedelic jam, and it almost felt like I was tripping. Just like the field in Holland some twenty-odd years earlier, I tried to resist. I had long ago decided I wasn't supposed to like this kind of music. Something about it was too happy…the vibes were too positive in a way that didn't mesh with all of my dark insanity. But I couldn't hold out, and for the first time in my life, I got what it was all about. I looked over at Darlin' and my sister's husband who hadn't smoked, and it was obvious they weren't really digging the whole scene. For some reason I found this very funny. Eventually I couldn't hold it in anymore. At first I just started giggling, but then began laughing out loud like a madman, completely and uncontrollably.

Before we left New York, my sister gave me a little bit of the Sour Diesel to take with me. The dad in me wasn't crazy about driving across state lines with weed in the car, but I knew I was going to want to smoke again, and there was little chance of me finding something of that caliber in Tennessee. Once we got on the road, I realized that after all of the years of traveling with drugs, having two kids in car seats was probably the best deterrent for trouble I'd ever had. Immediately after that, I regretted that I hadn't actually brought more.

***

After getting back home, I started planning the African safari. I had always wanted to go into the Congolese jungles, or deep into the vast Serengeti plains, but after a little research, I realized that South Africa would probably be more ideal for my mother. Despite some of the terrible shit the Dutch had brought down there, they also brought things like drivable roads and filtered water: the kind of infrastructure that makes traveling with a sixty-five-year-old woman a little less of a pain in the ass. Once it was settled, I went all out and found a private game reserve outside Kruger Park with some pretty luxurious accommodations and a good reputation for spotting game.

After I finished making all the plans and reservations, something that I had never done on any other trip I'd taken, I started to get the itch to smoke again. It had been a few weeks since the night of the Dead cover band, and I wanted to recreate the feeling I'd had at the show. I knew that so long as I wasn't smoking that often I could maintain a low tolerance, and really get the most out of the few grams I had. I picked up a little one-hitter at a head shop, and one evening after the kids were in bed I took a couple hits. I tried listening to a few tracks of the actual Dead, but it wasn't happening. I realized that whatever kind of magic they may have been able to achieve in a live setting, they never really figured out how to capture on record. "Sugar Magnolia" still made me feel a little nauseous. Since I was pumped up on all things African, I decided to put on some Fela Kuti and the Africa '70.

I had forgotten how good music could sound stoned, and even though I had just listened to the same record a week earlier, I started feeling those rhythmic grooves so deeply I almost started to cry.

Music had never lost its place in my heart as my first true love, but at some point I'd lost sight of just how transcendental it can actually be. I suddenly remembered how all of life's most simple truths—things that can't be expressed with mere words—can all be found within the rhythms of Africa. It is something physical, imprinted in our chromosomes. Alone in my bedroom, at 10:30 at night, I started dancing, like I was receiving communion from the gods.

When the record ended, I needed more. I put on "Palm Grease" from Herbie Hancock's *Thrust*, and then Sly's *Fresh*. Overwhelmed by rediscovering the magnitude and power of these recordings, I tried to think of what could satisfy my renewed and insatiable lust for the funk. I couldn't waste time with some bullshit—I needed a real fix. I was craving the heavy shit, something dirty, but deep. Tripped out, but rocking. My body, mind, and spirit were jonesing for something all-encompassing and I realized what I needed was Funkadelic. I put on *Standing on the Verge...*and within the first few bars, felt as if I was being released from the terrestrial shackles of my earthly existence and transported to the divine. Ecstatic with joy, it hit me like a holy orgasm. That all of these glorious sounds shared one common denominator could not be ignored: they all had roots in Africa.

★ ★ ✴

The trip from Tennessee to New York to Johannesburg to Cape Town was brutal. Cape Town turned out to be a great little city, but wasn't what I had flown halfway around the world for. One night we went out to hear some music at a place called Mama Africa, where some cats were doing their thing with marimbas. While I couldn't deny that it was kind of grooving, it wasn't quite what I was after. I was getting closer for sure, but knew the only way I'd really be able to get to the source of it all was to go deeper. It wasn't until we landed in Hoedspruit that I felt like I had finally arrived.

I could immediately feel that something was in the air…something about the way the electromagnetic particles were buzzing about, perhaps at a higher frequency than any of us are normally acclimated to. But although I had felt this in other places before, this was ground zero, where the entire wellspring of humanity originated. The place where mankind was born.

There was a taxi waiting to take us to a private lodge in the Balule Nature Reserve. Two minutes after getting into the car, we saw a giraffe just hanging out on the side of the road, eating some leaves off a tree. Not long after, we passed warthogs, kudu, and *springbokke*. We drove deep into the bush for almost an hour before we finally pulled into the lodge, and it was beautiful. Classic African buildings adorned with thatched roofs and furnished with hand-carved art and furniture made from native hardwoods; rustic, but equipped with all the amenities. Carefully designed to look and feel like a truly authentic African lodge, following specifications that would surely fulfill the most discerning imperial white man's dreams.

We were met by a welcoming committee of staff members armed with trays of cold cocktails and warm wet towels to clean our hands and faces. It was immediately obvious that there would be no way to remain anonymous, as if only pure random chance and coincidence had brought us all together. I decided right then and there that instead of allowing myself to succumb to a feeling of guilt and shame, I would participate in all of the indulgences and services provided, and would reciprocate their hospitality with an open wallet. As if the gods were inclined to indulge this hedonistic fantasy, there were only two other guests competing for the staff's impeccable attentiveness. Either that or we just got lucky, since it was technically considered the off-season.

They walked us over to our luxury hut, situated on the edge of the *veld* with a view so expansive we were able to see giraffes and zebras in the distance. They gave us a quick rundown of the camp rules, which all generally seemed designed to achieve the same objective: keeping the guests from being eaten. While I normally didn't like regimented schedules, I understood that a mauling or death probably wouldn't have looked that great on a brochure. They gave us a few minutes to get settled, and soon returned to escort us back to the dining area for a light lunch before our first excursion into the bush.

Right before we jumped into a dark green Land Rover, we were introduced to our guide and his tracker. For about an hour, we drove around without seeing anything, but it didn't really matter. Even if we had seen nothing more than the termite hills that dotted the scrub-filled landscape, we were all just happy to be there. After ten years of trying to *do the right thing*, it seemed I was finally able to enjoy the fruits of my labor. I felt deeply satisfied that it had all come full circle...that I was actually in a position to take my mother and sister on such an extravagant vacation. I had figured out a way to pull it all together and, for once, life was actually going my way.

The Land Rover suddenly stopped and our guide told us to be really quiet. At first, I wasn't sure what was happening—and then I saw him. Like an apparition, standing just a few feet away, was a massive African bull elephant, with full exquisite ivory tusks. The elephant has always been something of a spirit animal for me, and here I was face-to-face with the largest creature to still walk the earth. Within seconds, I realized he was not alone. There was a whole herd, over a dozen of them. In near silence, they walked right past us, so close you could have reached out and touched them.

After that, in the dusk of our first evening in the bush, it seemed as if all of the animals decided to come out just for us—more elephants, as well as rhinos, giraffes, and buffalo. We were even lucky enough to find the super elusive leopard. It was the height of the dry season, and typically considered the best time of year to view game, but it was way more than I ever could have expected. Over the next few days, we saw more animals than anyone could ever hope for. Zebras, giraffes, hippos, crocodiles, baboons, and even a pride of lions.

***

On one of our last mornings there, the day of my mom's birthday, our guide mentioned that he had to go into town to run a few errands. Since my sister had recently been dealing with some weird autoimmune thing that didn't allow her to drink, I asked him if he knew any place where he could grab a little weed for us. I suspected he would, so after he gave me a little smile, I handed him some cash.

I knew South Africa was known for a few strains like Swazi Gold and Durban Poison, but I wasn't in a position to be picky. I just wanted a little *dagga* or, as the Zulus called it, *insangu*. He returned right before our afternoon safari with a decent-sized bag of weed and some papers. I rolled up a few joints, and told my sister I had a surprise for her. To my disbelief, my mother didn't seem to mind, and I wound up smoking in front of her for the first time on her sixty-fifth birthday, in a Land Rover deep in the African bush. After we lit up, the tracker turned around and gave me a little nod, and I knew if he wasn't technically working, he would have gotten stoned with us too. What could beat getting baked out in the bush, with a bunch of wild animals all around?

When we got back to the lodge, feeling good and stoned, we met up with a new group of people who had just shown up in time for dinner. Under the stars, everyone was quietly enjoying a *braai* around an open fire, until someone decided to bring up the presidential election taking place in the States. Within five minutes, two of the new guests started arguing about which candidate was going to destroy or save our country. For at least a week, I had desperately hoped to avoid having to think about politics, and I promised myself I would not discuss it so long as I stood on African soil. But sure enough, their argument got more and more heated, until one of the staff members actually had to intervene. Thousands of miles from home, our divisions as a country were just as obvious abroad as they were in the States.

I started to feel that familiar tinge of stress creep slowly out of my nervous system and spread deep within the muscles of my back. It wasn't long before I couldn't take any more and decided I needed to leave the dining area to head back to the hut. When I got back, I sat down on the deck and looked out into the distance, watching the moon reflect off the Olifants River. I was lighting up another joint to try and cool off when I noticed a baboon standing less than thirty feet in front of me, watching me smoke in the dark.

Despite the fact that a baboon could run up

and rip off a limb, I did the one thing you are never supposed to do. Like some primate Svengali, it seemed as if he had put me in a trance. I couldn't help but sit there, totally still, staring deep into his eyes...when suddenly the landscape began to transform into a burning wasteland... as if I was being transported back into the waking nightmares of my youth. Out of the silence, I could hear the cries of a thousand million children, calling out to me in despair. I knew they needed my help, but I felt powerless. I closed my eyes and shook my head in a futile attempt to get the terrible visions out of my mind. I thought I had gotten past all of these apocalyptic hallucinations, and didn't understand how this could be happening to me again. I had come so far...

It had been well over a decade since I had last experienced anything like this, and I didn't want to believe what I was seeing. Overcome with fear, it felt like some terrible beast was watching me, and I was afraid to open my eyes. But then I remembered there actually *was* a beast staring at me, so I built up my courage and decided I had to face my fear.

And there it was. Standing practically face-to-face with me, looking deep into my eyes, was the baboon, except this time I noticed that something was different. Its body was the same, except the eyes and face were distorted. Somehow this new being looked familiar, and when that horrendous orange-skinned, yellow-haired primate finally came into perfect focus, I knew it was all real—this was no mere apparition or terrible dystopian *Planet of the Apes* vision of some distant future. This terrible beast had already begun sowing the seeds of our destruction: the madness was already in motion. I finally realized once and for all who this creature was—the monster that would be responsible for the end of civilization. This baboon was Donald Trump.

And then the reality of the situation hit me like a ton of bricks. It wasn't some maniacal demon mastermind that would be responsible for our undoing—it was us. I had to face the sad truth that it was not only our willingness to passively allow it, but our willingness to actually *support* the regime of some egotistical oligarch, a thin-skinned authoritarian with more money than brains, someone whose name we were actually going to commit to the ballot and vote for…that this baboon would hold the most powerful office in the world was beyond comprehension. But I knew it was true. I broke out in a cold sweat and began shivering in horror. Not because we were all too stupid to see the scam for what it really was, but because most of us didn't even seem to care. A large percentage of the American people were not only *ready* to watch the world burn, they were willing to help write the final chapter of our demise…just so long as they would be able to witness it and have front-row seats to the show. It was total insanity and, for the first time in my life, I felt like I was the one who was actually not crazy. And somehow that made it worse. Just when it felt like I was going to collapse from the sheer weight of this realization, I heard my sister call out my name. After I managed to snap myself out of my stupor, I realized the baboon was gone.

My sister told me that the staff had arranged something special, and that I should come back down to the fire. She said she thought they were going to put on some kind of show for my mother's birthday. I had seen enough performances that were designed strictly to entertain tourists, something to give the foreigners a little convoluted taste of culture, and I knew that they were almost always bad—but since it was for my mom, I agreed to follow her back. I walked down in silence, trying to come to terms with all that I had just seen: the final clear and definitive source of all of my nightmares. When I sat down, I ordered a glass of wine, and in an attempt to drown away the sorrow, swallowed it in one gulp.

The staff shuffled in a line down to the fire, and were humming some tune so faintly, it could barely be heard. They were not wearing any animal skins or headdresses; no one was carrying any spears or shields; they just had on their normal work clothes. They were not some troupe of professional performers, shipped in for the sole purpose of entertaining the guests; these were just the regular employees of the lodge. Their solemn hymn became louder and louder in what seemed to be a perfectly synchronized rhythm, beating in complete unison with my heart. Aside from the sound of their feet stomping lightly on the ground, there was no instrumentation, but, after a few moments, one of them suddenly broke from the chant and began singing the sweetest, most melancholy and hauntingly beautiful melody I have ever heard. Her voice filled the air in a perfect combination of joy and pain, and despite not being able to understand the words, I knew that they contained all the truths of the world that anyone could ever hope to learn.

And finally, I understood...that even if the planet *was* on the brink of absolute destruction, the cosmos will never function in absolutes. For every action, there is a reaction; and for every terrible act that could ever be committed, there would always be a responding act of beauty and grace. It didn't matter that I had just seen a tremendous wave of pain and suffering—for I knew that at some point all of us were destined to suffer. What mattered was the way in which we chose to live. Because in the end all of us will need to take responsibility not only for our own lives, but for the lives of us all. Only then, when the world *does* end in nuclear annihilation, can we take solace in knowing there will at least be one final burst of glorious blinding light.

Yet despite all of this...this beautiful African angel continued to sing her song, and somehow I knew that no matter what could ever happen, everything was going to be all right.

Joseph Davida

GLOSSARY

Baksheesh: Typically a "tip" or a bribe in the Middle East and Asia.
Bang Kwang: Prison in Thailand.
Bango: Middle Eastern grass (for smoking).
Bodega: Hispanic grocery store.
Botánica: Store that sells candles, amulets, and Santeria spells.
Burka: Muslim head covering.
Chillum: A clay cylinder used a pipe.
Dagga: South African word for "marijuana."
Fin: Opium in Thai.
Farang: Thai word for foreigner.
Kabouters: Dutch elves and gnomes.
Gaijin: Japanese word for foreigner.
Haji: Japanese word for "shame."
Hajj: Islamic pilgrimage.
Hara-kiri: Suicide method used by the Samurai.
Insagu: Zulu word for "marijuana."
Kathoey: Thai word for transvestite.
Kufiya: Head scarf used in the Middle East.
La shukran: "No thanks" in Arabic.
Mandala: A geometric pattern used for visual meditation.
Manhout: Someone who takes care of, trains, and rides elephants.
Mantra: A series of words that are repeated over and over to clear the mind during meditation.
Rumspringa: A time for Amish adolescents to leave their communities and experience freedom from their church. Usually for a year to decide if they would like to stay away or return to be baptized.
Sadhu: Hindu holy man.
Sakoku: Japanese period of self-imposed isolation from 1633 to 1866.
Salat/salah: Islamic prayers, performed five times daily.
Souk: Middle Eastern market or bazaar.
Stela (plural *stelae*): An upright stone slab typically bearing a relief design.
Stupa: The dome-shaped steeple of a Buddhist temple.
Thankas: Buddhist paintings.
Tika powder: Red powder usually used to mark foreheads, and statues for holy ceremonies.
Tuk tuk: Motorized rickshaw.
Veld: A vast plain in Africa.
Wai Khru tattoos: Traditional religious tattoos usually done by a Buddhist monk with a stick in Thailand.
Ya-Ba: Cheap speed popular in Asia.

CPSIA information can be obtained
at www.ICGtesting.com
Printed in the USA
FFOW02n0923160518
46704082-48819FF